Christians in a
PC World

'Political correctness in western countries has taken on a distinctly anti-Christian tinge in recent years. John Benton exposes this development to clear, biblical analysis and helps us to see the seriousness of its implications in the key areas of sexuality, pluralism and feminism. Christians today need to grasp what these shifts in thinking mean for them and for their faith — this book will help you do just that.'

Robert Strivens, Principal, London Theological Seminary

'This well-documented and carefully argued handbook helps us to understand what has happened to our culture and why, what today's real issues are and how to bring biblical revelation to bear on our contemporary challenges. I hope that it will be widely read and that this important contribution will generate thought, debate and action among Christians on these crucial matters.'

David Jackman, Past President of the Proclamation Trust

'John Benton has given us a most helpful primer on political correctness and its implications for Christian thought and life. Reading his book has had the effect of developing my understanding, refining my convictions, and refuelling my hope in the unique gospel of Jesus Christ. Benton's concern for the loss of both objective discourse and a moral framework ends up providing a clear call for people to face the stark reality of the intellectual bondage of political correctness. In the end, Benton has shown us what life is like when we ignore God.'

Mike Bullmore, Senior Pastor of Crossway Community Church, Kenosha, Wisconsin, USA; and a Council Member for *The Gospel Coalition*

'If you've ever longed for clarity on just how far Western postmodern culture has moved from the straight and defined lines of the Christian faith, John Benton's Christians in a PC World *is for you. John writes with equal parts of wisdom and winsomeness as he addresses some of the most significant streams of non- and anti-Christian developments in recent years. Especially helpful is his discussion of just how evangelicals have fallen prey to the wiles of this ever-pressing PC culture. To understand better the peril of our times* and the contrasting beauty of God's good and wise ways, one will benefit greatly by thinking carefully through the pages of this marvellously lucid and faithful study.'

Bruce A. Ware, Professor of Christian Theology, The Southern Baptist
Theological Seminary, Louisville, Kentucky, USA

'This is essential reading for every Christian who wishes to understand what is going on in the world around them. The book is well-researched, informative and disturbing. We are indebted to John Benton for his picture of Western society today, for warning evangelical churches not to compromise the gospel and for showing, from a thoroughly biblical perspective, how Christians can best live out their lives and evangelize in the contemporary situation.'

Philip Eveson
retired minister, Kensit Evangelical Church, London

Christians in a
PC World

by

John Benton

 Books

EP BOOKS
Faverdale North
Darlington
DL3 0PH, England

www.epbooks.org
e-mail: sales@epbooks.org

EP books are distributed in the USA by:
JPL Fulfillment, 3741 Linden Avenue Southeast, Grand Rapids, MI 49548

e-mail: orders@jplfulfillment.com
Tel: 877.683.6935

First published 2013

British Library Cataloguing in Publication Data available

ISBN: 978-085-234-9120

Contents

For
Freddie Benton, Evie Benton
Bethan Foster, Adah Benton

'I had forgotten that,' said Eomer. 'It is hard to be
sure of anything among so many marvels.
The world is all grown strange...
How shall a man judge what to do in such times?'

'As he has ever judged,' said Aragorn.
'Good and ill have not changed since yesteryear;
nor are they one thing among Elves and Dwarves
and another among Men.
It is a man's part to discern them,
as much in the Golden Wood as in his own house'

J. R. R. Tolkien: The Lord of the Rings

Introduction

Listen to a writer, Anthony Browne, a Cambridge graduate and not long ago the Europe correspondent for *The Times* newspaper:

> For centuries Britain has been a beacon of liberty of thought, belief and speech in the world, but now its intellectual and political life is in chains. Members of the public, academics, journalists and politicians are afraid of thinking certain thoughts. People are vilified if they publicly diverge from accepted beliefs, sacked or even investigated by the police for crimes against received wisdom. Whole areas of debate have been closed down by the crushing dominance of the moralistic ideology of political correctness. (*The Retreat of Reason*)

What kind of thing is he talking about?

For example, I have a friend who is a Christian and has a political life as a local councillor. During 2012 as the Coalition Government canvassed their desire to redefine marriage so as to include gay relationships, a debate was called for on the subject at the town's council. Although the issue had nothing whatever to do with the areas of jurisdiction relating to a town council, nevertheless it was decided that out of courtesy a debate should be allowed. A large group of supporters for the redefinition of marriage, around forty to fifty people turned up. A number of short speeches from those representing the gay lobby were heard in respectful silence. But as my friend, who took a different point of view, got up to speak there was hissing and heckling. What my friend had to say was drowned in a torrent of abuse. Rational debate was impossible. It simply came down to intimidation. Later my friend received a number of abusive emails which were very upsetting.

Another example of the kind of thing Anthony Browne is talking about would be the implementation of the Sexual Orientation Regulations which came into force in 2007. Because of those regulations adoption agencies which were unable in good conscience to place children with same-sex couples were closed down. That was the case even when other agencies were available for same-sex couples to adopt children. This is not a 'live and let live' approach to life. This is people's consciences simply being set aside.

Not just about sex

But lest we think this is all to do with attitudes to sex, let me mention a different example. Just a few years ago we celebrated the bicentenary of the abolition of the slave trade in Britain. There was something of a commemoration of the work of the great Christian politician William Wilberforce and his major contribution in stopping slavery. But although European culpability in the enslavement of Africans from the seventeenth to the nineteenth century was rightly highlighted by the British media, the Islamic world's involvement with slavery, including the enslavement of Africans and, to a lesser extent, Europeans, was hardly mentioned. This happened even though in many areas of the world Islamic slavery is still going on today. (One thinks of the work of Baroness Cox and others freeing slaves in the Sudan.) Why was this? Why were Europeans (rightly) castigated, but relatively little was said on the major TV channels about Muslim involvement with slavery? It is because it would have been considered politically incorrect to challenge Islam. Somehow, though injustices by Westerners are fair game for criticism, to raise the same questions about the behaviour of other groups is frowned upon.

This is the abandoning of an objective approach. It is very different from the British sense of even-handedness and fair play of previous years.

The PC world

The world has changed. Political correctness (PC) now holds tremendous sway. We live in a 'PC' world. We will give attention to a specific definition of political correctness later. But broadly speaking, political correctness is a setting aside of freedom of speech in the name of equality and not upsetting certain groups of people.

The old framework of British justice is no longer what it once was, and Christians need to understand this change of environment. A whole new set of rules has begun to apply in the way society runs. There is no longer a level playing-field. And more than that, politically correct campaigners would argue that it is right that the playing-field is no longer level. Furthermore, not only is this new outlook putting pressure on many churches, it is also causing some churches and church leaders to compromise and even rewrite the gospel.

This book is an attempt, from a Biblical point of view, to get our heads around what is happening and what it may mean for Christians in the future.

Chapter 1
Atheism and its consequences

In this first chapter, I want to set the scene of contemporary society in the West generally, but especially in the UK, and sketch out briefly the foundational change in society which has led to the rise of political correctness.

Some years ago the then Archbishop of Canterbury, Lord Carey, described Britain as a place w1here a 'tacit atheism' has come to dominate people's thinking. In the census of 2001, 70% of the population of England and Wales described themselves as Christians. By 2011 that figure had fallen to 59%. That is still quite a high proportion of the population. Nevertheless, Lord Carey's comment is true. When it comes to everyday life most people do not see God to be relevant. Sentimentally, there may be an attachment to a 'Christian' ethic, by which most people mean the so-called 'golden rule' of 'doing to others what you would have them do to you' based on Jesus' words in Matthew 7.12. However, what they mean by that is generally a moral neutrality which is very different from what Christ intended[1]. But when it comes to daily life, in practice, belief in God is not taken seriously.

The Bible would describe this move towards tacit atheism as 'forgetting God'. Although those who peddle ideas of the non-existence or irrelevance of God like to give the impression that they are very modern, *avant-garde* and daringly radical in their outlook, actually fallen human nature's tendency to atheism was being addressed by the writers of the Bible over three thousand years ago. It does not take God by surprise.

Nothing new

There is nothing new about atheism. King David famously said in his Psalms that it is the fool who says in his heart 'There is no God' (Ps. 14:1; 53:1). He was writing around a thousand years before Christ. And interestingly, some five hundred years before David, Moses explained one of the primary reasons for 'forgetting God'. He warned the people of Israel about this. He told them that once they entered the Promised Land they would become prosperous. The land God was giving them to live in was such a fertile place that their labour would produce much more than they needed and they would become well-off. Then they would be tempted towards tacit atheism. Prosperity gives us the illusion of human independence. With plenty of resources, the Israelites would be seduced into thinking that they no longer needed God. Listen to Moses' warning in his farewell message to his people recorded in Deuteronomy 8:11-18:

> [11]Be careful that you do not forget the LORD your God, failing to observe his commands, his laws and his decrees that I am giving you this day. [12]Otherwise, when you eat and are satisfied, when you build fine houses and settle down, [13]and when your herds and flocks grow large and your silver and gold increase and all you have is multiplied, [14]then your heart will become proud and you will forget the LORD your God, who brought you out of Egypt, out of the land of slavery. [15]He led you

through the vast and dreadful wilderness, that thirsty and waterless land, with its venomous snakes and scorpions. He brought you water out of hard rock. [16]He gave you manna to eat in the wilderness, something your ancestors had never known, to humble and test you so that in the end it might go well with you. [17]You may say to yourself, 'My power and the strength of my hands have produced this wealth for me.' [18]But remember the LORD your God, for it is he who gives you the ability to produce wealth, and so confirms his covenant, which he swore to your ancestors, as it is today.

Much has changed in Western society over the last half-century or so. For a start, generally speaking, we have become far more wealthy than, say, many of our grandparents were. The increase in wealth has also gone hand-in-hand with the rise of wonderful technology and medicine. So it is, just as Moses warned, that people feel that they no longer need God. They can stand on their own two feet, thank you very much. All their needs for life are addressed. Modern people have a house and a car and money in the bank. If they are ill, there is the NHS. If they are unhappy or need cheering up, there is always the TV or the internet. 'What do I need God for?' they ask themselves – forgetting that it is God who gave them life in the first place, the resources of the earth, and the ability to work and think and become prosperous.

This connection between atheism and material prosperity has been traced by academics. For example, in her book *Holding Up A Mirror: How Civilizations Decline*, Anne Glyn-Jones explains the findings of the Russian-American thinker Pitirim Sorokin. Sorokin classified societies according to their 'cultural mentality' – that is, the way they think about the world. He said that these can be 'ideational' (reality is spiritual), 'sensate' (reality is material), or 'idealistic' (a synthesis of the two). He suggested that major civilizations evolve from an ideational, to an idealistic, and eventually to a sensate mentality. The 'sensate' way of thinking is basically that of the materialist, the atheist. Each of these phases of cultural development not only seeks to describe the nature of reality, but also stipulates the nature of human needs and goals to be satisfied. Sorokin interpreted the contemporary Western civilisation as a sensate civilisation dedicated to technological progress, and prophesied its fall into decadence.

To put his theory of the decline of civilizations simply, Sorokin said that society requires a moral framework in order to function in a stable way. The authority of morality has always been derived from a sense of the divine or the supernatural. It is religious in essence. However, here a dynamic begins to come into play. The proper functioning of a stable society produces economic prosperity. But as this grows, it tends to influence people to think that the material world is all that really matters. From here, society feels that it does not need religion or a sense of the divine. This undermines the authority of moral standards, and so leads eventually to the destruction of the very social stability which caused the society to prosper in the first place. Sorokin's work sought to trace this trajectory in the rise and fall of civilizations such as those of ancient Greece and ancient Rome, as well as others. So he too would not be surprised at the denial of God in the prosperous contemporary West.

As we shall see, it is from this tacit atheism and its corresponding impact on ideas of morality that the whole confusion over fairness and the rise of political correctness has flowed.

The secular experiment

So, given the affluence in which we live, it is not surprising that the UK has been involved in a grand social experiment to see what life is like when we ignore God. This may or may not have been embarked on deliberately, but nevertheless it is a fair description of what has been happening. We have become a secular society. The vast majority of people have been persuaded that God either does not exist or counts for nothing in their lives.

Since approximately the 1960s, God has been marginalised. We have decided that we do not need him. So, we have turned the UK into a gigantic nationwide laboratory to see what happens to life when God is sidelined. Now, after half a century or so, the results are coming in.

Once again it is fascinating to find that the Bible anticipates where all this would lead. The state of the UK and the direction it is taking seem almost inevitable to Bible-believing Christians. What we see happening around us is precisely what the apostle Paul said would happen when people suppress the truth about God. Here are his words in Romans 1:

> [18]The wrath of God is being revealed from heaven against all the godlessness and wickedness of men who suppress the truth by their wickedness, [19]since what may be known about God is plain to them, because God has made it plain to them. [20]For since the creation of the world God's invisible qualities—his eternal power and divine nature—have been clearly seen, being understood from what has been made, so that men are without excuse.

[21]For although they knew God, they neither glorified him as God nor gave thanks to him, but their thinking became futile and their foolish hearts were darkened. [22]Although they claimed to be wise, they became fools [23]and exchanged the glory of the immortal God for images made to look like mortal man and birds and animals and reptiles.

[24]Therefore God gave them over in the sinful desires of their hearts to sexual impurity for the degrading of their bodies with one another. [25]They exchanged the truth of God for a lie, and worshipped and served created things rather than the Creator—who is forever praised. Amen. [26]Because of this, God gave them over to shameful lusts. Even their women exchanged natural relations for unnatural ones. [27]In the same way the men also abandoned natural relations with women and were inflamed with lust for one another. Men committed indecent acts with other men, and received in themselves the due penalty for their perversion.

[28]Furthermore, since they did not think it worthwhile to retain the knowledge of God, he gave them over to a depraved mind, to do what ought not to be done. [29]They have become filled with every kind of wickedness, evil, greed and depravity. They are full of envy, murder, strife, deceit and malice. They are gossips, [30]slanderers, God-haters, insolent, arrogant and boastful; they invent ways of doing evil; they disobey their parents; [31]they are senseless, faithless, heartless, ruthless. [32]Although they know God's righteous decree that those who do such things deserve death, they not only continue to do these very things but also approve of those who practise them.

The outline of the logic of these verses is as follows. Paul argues that God's wrath is justifiably revealed because people trample on and deny the truth about the one true God. They replace him in their lives by various idols (verses 18-23). Then in verses 24-32 he specifies the consequences of this in terms of the moral disintegration of human society.

We are told in verse 18 that 'The wrath of God is being revealed from heaven against all the godlessness and wickedness of men who suppress the truth by their wickedness.' It all begins with fallen humanity suppressing the truth about God. Our failure is only secondarily moral. Primarily, it is spiritual. It stems from 'godlessness'; in other words, living without God. This is precisely what pertains in our society today. We have forgotten God. We have rejected him. We deny his existence.

Why is God revealing his wrath? The answer is because the knowledge of God is evident through the design of creation (verse 20), and through the moral sense written into us by which we judge everything including each other (verse 32).

Instead of acknowledging what is blindingly obvious, that human beings and our world are so beautifully and wonderfully made that there must be a Designer, we prefer to take the mathematically nonsensical view that it all came about by myriads of chance collisions of fundamental particles which originated out of absolutely nothing.

When it comes to moral judgements, those of a liberal outlook criticise those on the right and *vice versa*. Having to live with a huge national debt, we all deplore what bankers and politicians have done. We feel a righteous indignation. Instead of recognising that there must be a moral law-giver of whose standards we are aware (and we assume that those whom we are criticising must be aware of them too), we prefer to believe (illogically) that there is no Judge to whom we are answerable. Deep down we know that there are absolutes of right and wrong independent of ourselves: otherwise, what would be the point of criticising others? But we deny the idea even though we know it is true.

Despite such evidences of God confronting us daily, people suppress the truth (verse 18) and exchange the truth of God for a lie (verse 25).

God-forsaken?

Romans 1 tells us that 'the wrath of God is being revealed'. That is in the present tense. How, in the present, does God express his wrath against us when we suppress the truth about him?

It is rarely through apocalyptic catastrophes. Instead, the apostle Paul tells us that God gives us over to the fruit of godlessness. He abandons us to the consequences. There is a threefold repetition of the phrase 'God gave them over.' In verse 24 we read 'Therefore God gave them over in the sinful desires of their hearts to sexual impurity for the degrading of their bodies with one another.' In verse 26 we find 'Because of this, God gave them over to shameful lusts. Even their women exchanged natural relations for unnatural ones.' In verse 28 Paul writes, 'Furthermore, since they did not think it worthwhile to retain the knowledge of God, he gave them over to a depraved mind, to do what ought not to be done'.

The apostle emphasizes two particular results of being God-forsaken. It leads to foolishness and decadence. And in our land of tacit atheism we see precisely those things.

22

Decadence and foolishness

For me, this is another large piece of contemporary evidence for the truth of Christianity. Many secular humanists in the past argued that God was irrelevant and that it would be perfectly possible to have a godless society which was decent, moral and upright.

If the experiment of 'life without God' in which we have been engaged since the 1960s had resulted in a decent, upright society with no rise in family breakdown, sexual perversion, drunkenness and violence on our streets at night, etc., then Romans 1 would have been wrong and the Christian faith called into question. But that has not been the result at all. In fact, the contrary has been the case. We have simply seen Romans 1 come to life before our eyes. Family breakdown, drug abuse, street violence, drunkenness, sexually transmitted diseases, the prisons overflowing and the justice system not able to cope; these things and many more are common. But I do not want to major on that here.

Paul sees foolishness as the initial result of atheism. Without God, we fall into stupidity. Verses 21-23 tell us, 'For although they knew God, they neither glorified him as God nor gave thanks to him, but their thinking became futile and their foolish hearts were darkened. Although they claimed to be wise, they became fools and exchanged the glory of the immortal God for images made to look like mortal man and birds and animals and reptiles.' Whether it is primitive tribes worshipping 'sacred' stones in some faraway forest or contemporary Westerners living for their careers or their latest sexual encounter or the buzz they get from new technology, we all fall into making something that is less than ourselves the thing we live for. This indicates that something has gone

23

very wrong with the way we are thinking. It signals that we are living a life that does not make sense.

Ultimate Questions

Let me just try to spell this out this foolishness for a moment. The three great questions about life, which all the philosophers have toiled over, are the questions of origins (where we came from), morality (how we should live) and knowledge (truth and how we can know it). The answers to the last two depend on the answer to the first one. But the atheist has no answers – or, at least, no rational and sensible answers to these questions.

Origins
If we ask 'Where did the universe come from?' the atheist has four possible responses. *First*, it has always existed. This option is now seen as a non-starter (forgive the humour), largely as a result of the discoveries of modern science, which point very definitely to the universe having some kind of beginning. *Second*, it came from absolutely nothing. We can immediately dismiss this as nonsense. Something cannot possibly come from nothing. If we think that, we might as well throw away our brains. *Third*, it came from a kind of 'nothing' but which is actually a certain package of energy and physical laws. But if you take that route you have not solved the problem because then you must not ask where that package came from. You have simply pushed the question a step back. *Fourth*, the only response left to the atheist is that you are not allowed to ask the question. In other words, they have no reasonable answer. In the area of origins we are left with foolishness.

Morality
If the basis of everything is mere time, chance and energy

24

the moral realm has no ultimate reality. It is a purely human construct. So it is up to you how you want to live. For some people morality is individual – 'be true to yourself'. For others it must be social – whatever the majority thinks is right – though of course the masses can be swayed by the media. There is no answer to how you should live. What people thought fifty years ago on many issues is now considered wrong. Morality becomes relativized. So we ask, for example, why the West thinks it has the right to impose its values on other cultures? Nearer to home, we ask: why shouldn't gay couples be allowed to marry if they want to? If someone wants to commit suicide, why shouldn't they be allowed to do it? Starting from an atheistic position, there are no definite answers to moral questions. It follows that there are no universal values. It actually means (though our society would not like to admit this) that ideas such as equality, justice and human rights which ought to apply to everyone have no foundation. Logically, even acts of evil such as genocide or a government telling deliberate lies can no longer be called 'evil' in any absolute sense. The whole basis of what we call civilized society is swept away. This is foolishness.

Truth

The victors always write the history! Someone who is labelled a terrorist by one group is called a freedom fighter by another. What is the truth? It depends where you are standing. If there is no absolute law, or law-maker, then there is no way of deciding. It all becomes simply a matter of opinion. More than that, Christians believe that God made human beings in his own image and gave us minds capable of knowing reality, parallel to the way he does. But without God, knowledge and language are merely human constructs. They can only represent what is going on in our minds subjectively. There is no guarantee that what is going on in our minds actually relates to objective reality. If that is the case, what is truth? We can never be sure we know the truth. But of course, none of us live in total uncertainty. We live as if we know what is true. Once again, we are brought back to a contradiction.

Hence we see that atheism leaves us with foolishness. Thus we have a professed atheist like Alain de Botton publishing his book *Religion for Atheists*, which is in fact simply an exercise in lamenting all the elements of civilized living which no longer make sense and go by the board in a godless world. He even bemoans the moral 'freedom' which atheists have fought to gain. 'We have grown sick of being left to do as we please,' he says (page 77). 'Our deepest wish may be that someone should come along and save us from ourselves' (page 72).

With no basis for right and wrong, and no certainty about truth and error, everything in life becomes a matter of opinion. This is known as relativism. You see it one way, I see it in another, but there is no correct or incorrect way. Here we find the open door through which political correctness enters. It is against that background that the idea of saying that what someone else is doing is 'wrong' or that we have a 'better' way of doing things is deemed offensive and unacceptable. This is the logic which has led us into a world ruled by political correctness. Feminists see things one way, chauvinists another. People of one religion have one view on suicide bombing, whereas people of another religion or no religion have another view. There is no right answer. In fact, it is arrogant to believe that you have the right answer. That, broadly speaking, is how the tacit atheism of the Western world has brought us to where we are.

Repudiating atheism

Obviously there is a huge amount that could be said concerning why atheism is wrong. In particular, we have already noted from Romans 1 the witness to God in creation and in the inbuilt sense of right and wrong in the human conscience. But let me just say three things.

Practically

We can see the 'foolishness' which tacit atheism brings beginning to work out in our own land. Without God, there are no answers to the great questions of existence. The highest purpose we can have is to make personal choice, self-fulfilment and 'enjoying ourselves' our 'trinitarian' deity. But in so doing we are turned into fools, says Romans 1. Think of the plain evidence which all the research shows for the benefits of traditional marriage and family life to the whole of society. Think of the explosion of sexually transmitted diseases; and of street crime by fatherless boys, which is verging on becoming unmanageable. Yet can our society say, 'Hey, we have got this wrong. We had better get back to promoting the family and sexual fidelity'? Of course not, because it would offend the great god of 'personal choice'. Thus we carry on in our foolishness.

Theoretically

We need to note that in stating the conclusion that, for example, 'There is no such thing as truth' you are stating a contradiction, because you are claiming that it is true that there is no such thing as truth. This in itself should be enough to ring alarm bells with us. This kind of stance is inviting us to believe a contradiction. No one can live consistently with the implications of atheism. The great atheist Friedrich Nietzsche said, 'What is truth…truths are illusions about which one has forgotten that this is what they are.' But in saying that he was stating what he thought was true; and true for everyone! This is foolishness. And no one lives like that in the real world. As we have already indicated, people, even atheists, live as if they can know the truth. For example, they live knowing the truth about how much money there is in their bank account, and they want there to be no errors or misleading information concerning their balance. Or again, since we are beginning to think about political correctness, what is the great characteristic of so many politically correct people? They take the moral high ground and decry others. They tell us to take down Christmas decorations in our cities because they might offend the Muslims – even when many reasonable Muslims say they are not at all offended. But nevertheless political correctness insists because it knows better! But we are taught that all viewpoints are equally valid – especially moral and religious ones. So why do we have to take down Christmas decorations which speak of the birth of Jesus? This shows total inconsistency. And it leads us to think that if this is where we end up starting from the basic premise of atheism, then it seems to indicate that the basic premise itself is wrong.

Personally
We have been engaged in the great experiment of seeing what life is like without God – which has led us at present to the enormous influence of political correctness. But back in 1994 the novelist Douglas Coupland, famous for his iconic book *Generation X*, wrote another book with the title *Life After God*. It caused quite a stir. Here is someone who was living in the light of tacit atheism, and struggling to explain what he felt. Interestingly, he concludes the book in this way:

> Now – here is my secret: I tell it to you with an openness
> of heart I doubt I shall ever achieve again, so I pray

that you are in a quiet room as you hear these words. My secret is that I need God – that I am sick and can no longer make it alone. I need God to help me give, because I no longer seem capable of giving; to help me to be kind, as I am no longer capable of kindness; to help me love, as I seem beyond being able to love.

If he means what he appears to say, that is quite a devastating admission. Coupland is saying is that he needs God personally. He needs God in order to make him really human and to enable him to love others. It is only belief in God which can guarantee true humanity. Tacit atheism and the political correctness which flows from it are making us increasingly into a lost and disorientated society.

[1] Christ intended the 'golden rule' to be a summary of 'the Law and the Prophets'. It tells us how to treat each other given the framework of, for example, the Ten Commandments. But as modern society has rejected God's commandments, the 'golden rule' has degenerated into simply doing our best to please others and make no moral judgements.

Chapter 2
A briefing on post-modernism

Over the period of one generation our society has changed dramatically. At the root of much of the change has been the acceptance of tacit atheism, which has led to the rise of what is called the post-modern world-view. We need to understand something of this if we are to live and speak for Christ effectively in the contemporary world.

In terms of the previous chapter we can see post-modernism (PM) as a consequence of atheism. Though this is a very dismissive statement (and I do not mean to be dismissive, for I am well aware that serious and complex issues are involved), nevertheless, post-modernism has to be subsumed under that category of 'foolishness' which (as Paul explains) results when a society suppresses the truth about God. And political correctness, as we shall see, is linked to the post-modern outlook. PM is really the mother of PC. It is the environment in which political correctness has been created and found plausibility. So a brief look at post-modernism will help us.

Post-modernism has also crept into certain areas of the church and has subtly undermined the gospel. We will consider this a little more fully in later chapters. But for the moment, in order to defend the truth and to have a healthy understanding of many of today's secular opponents of the gospel, we need to be aware of post-modernism.

What is post-modernism?

The 'post' in post-modernism indicates that we are living in times which are somehow 'after' the modern era. It sounds like linguistic nonsense; whatever is current is by definition modern. But the word 'modern' is being used in a different sense here.

Modern refers to 'modernism'. This refers to the outlook of the philosophical Enlightenment which emerged in seventeenth- and eighteenth-century continental Europe. Fostered by the well-off in places like France, the Enlightenment idolized human reason. All the world's problems could be solved through common sense, logical thinking and the application of science. The Enlightenment believed that man had 'come of age', and no longer required belief in God. It was secular and materialistic. Human logic and the scientific method could establish truth and would produce a good and just society in which people would be free and fulfilled. It was this vision which drove forward the Western world in its technology throughout the nineteenth century, and sustained a great humanistic optimism concerning the future.

But this optimistic vision of modernism is now seen as a failure and is being rejected by our society. Though the twentieth century began with great expectations of human progress, soon the two world wars, harnessing all the fruits of technology and climaxing in the horror of the atomic bombs unleashed on Japan, brought many people to sober reflection. What had we really achieved? The old certainty that rational people can, with perseverance, eventually disentangle all the mess mankind finds itself in began to fall apart. This led to the emergence of the post-modern outlook.

Post-modernism is about an abandonment of the 'modern vision'. It sets aside reason and universal truth in favour of 'truth' which can only be known personally. There are three crucial elements here.

- *First*, PM rejects absolute truth in favour of thorough-going relativism. It is reminiscent of that famous verse in the book of Judges which says that because there was no king (no absolute ruler) 'everyone did what was right in his own eyes' (Judg. 21:25, NKJV). PM rejects the old sovereign, 'king' reason. It believes that reason alone cannot establish universal truth. Reason is a process which will lead in different directions depending on one's assumptions. Often one's assumptions are prior commitments which are based on ephemeral emotions or different cultural backgrounds.

- *Second*, with this in mind, PM sees reality as incoherent and fragmented. This is because there is no universal truth by which to measure or put in order pieces of information. Therefore PM rejects the idea of any overarching explanation of our world (meta-narrative). There is no story to our world. PM rejects not only religious explanations, but also the scientific meta-narrative. After all, it seems as though scientific theories keep changing all the time as new discoveries are made. Once we believed in a Newtonian universe, then, along came Einstein. Who knows whose theories will be at the top of the pile next?

- *Third*, PM sees all truth claims as simply power-plays on the part of various groups or individuals, designed to manipulate other people. It is most important to realise this. Truth has no reality. It is just a tool used by intelligent and forceful people to push others around. This means that perpetrators of what they call 'the truth' are actually oppressors and turn other people whom they persuade of their convictions into victims of their thinking. To press 'the truth' is to enslave others. This gives an aggressiveness to many post-modern thinkers, who feel that they are 'freedom fighters' in the realm of ideas. And because there is, in their terms, no truth (or morality), they see it as perfectly legitimate to use any tactics to undermine those who seek to stand for truth. So if they cannot out-argue their opponents, then slander or merely shouting them down is considered justifiable. We are seeing more and more of this from pressure groups in contemporary politics. Intimidation of opponents, either in political meetings or via the social media, is considered legitimate.

This might seem quite bizarre to those of us educated to believe in historical, moral and scientific truth, within a school syllabus which was fundamentally 'modern'. But this 'modern' outlook is being rejected.

No surprise

However, the failure of modernism should not surprise us as Christians. We know that Christ alone is the source of truth and life. Jesus said 'I am the way and the truth and the life' (John 14:6; cf. Rom.1:21-22; 1 Cor. 1:20). The Bible is all for science and history. But it does warn us that any system of knowledge which ignores God is bound to be incomplete and to be fundamentally flawed. The world is held together by God's word. The modern project was to set up a totally 'objective' and impersonal approach to knowing, using finite man as its starting-point. But the truth is that reality, though accessible to us, is far bigger than we can grasp. Jesus, the Son of God, alone knows all truth and is the truth.

Since God (the maker of all things) is real, the material universe is not self-contained or self-explanatory. Because God is real, and not a figment of our imaginations, truth is objective. But because God is personal (indeed tri-personal in the persons of the Trinity), that truth must be personal too. Thus there is truth in both the 'modern' and 'post-modern' approaches to reality. But these can only be properly brought together within a Christian framework. They can only find proper harmony in the light of the objective and personal Creator of all. This, in a nutshell, is why both free-standing modernism and subjective post-modernism fail.

Why the change to PM?

Post-modernism is a loveable but unworkable lie. It is loveable to us as self-centred sinners, because it means we can make our own 'truth'. But it is unworkable because it rejects the idea of truth. Nevertheless, it has taken hold. Why is that? It has done so for many different reasons which came together during the twentieth century. For example…

At the theoretical level, the post-modern outlook has been facilitated by the undermining of language through what is known as 'deconstructionism'. Influential thinkers like Michel Foucault (1926-84) and Jacques Derrida (1930-2004), say that human language does not refer to an objective world 'out there', but is a self-referential system of signs (ultimately peculiar to the individual) which is basically meaningless in any absolute sense. Actually, as we have already seen, post-modernism would say that language does not convey truth, but is simply a means of seeking to exercise power over other people.

As Bible-believing Christians, we would need to disagree with this view of language. God himself, not man, is the first one to speak in Scripture. Language is not a purely human construct (cf. Gen. 1:5, 8, etc.; 2:19-20, 23). But rejecting the idea of God (who is the source of universal truth) as the creator of human language, and language therefore being able to serve truth, gives deconstructionism its opportunity.

Here is an example of deconstruction which I came across. It indicates how a statement can be shown to mean quite the opposite of what it appears to say, and hence to be meaningless. The American Declaration of Independence states: 'We hold these truths to be self-evident, that all men are created equal; that they are endowed by their Creator with certain unalienable rights; that among these are life, liberty and the pursuit of happiness.'

This can be deconstructed, they would say, along the following lines:

- Although the text speaks of equality, its language excludes women ('all men are created equal').
- Although it speaks of liberty, its author, Thomas Jefferson, owned slaves.
- So the surface meaning of equality and liberty is contradicted by the subtext.
- It enshrines the rights of the wealthy white males who signed it, grounding their privilege in God.
- The Declaration of Independence is thus deconstructed into just another power play, implying the opposite of its surface meaning.

In this way, post-modernism tells us that language cannot be trusted, and therefore any 'truth' which that language claims to express is unreliable. This is seen as a death blow to 'modernism'.

<u>At the popular level</u>, the causes of this shift to post-modernism are probably too complex to analyse easily. But let me suggest a few reasons, some of which we have already touched on.

- The Enlightenment was wedded to the 'meta-narrative' given by science. But lately many people have come to the conclusion that science and technology have created as many problems as they have solved. We can think of nuclear bombs, the petrol engine and the pollution of the environment, global warming, etc. So science and scientific truth have fallen from favour with many people.

- Ideologies purporting to be 'the truth' have produced much harm in the world as their followers have tried to impose 'the truth' on other people. Religion has been prepared to burn heretics and murder 'infidels' and declare *jihad* against others. Atheistic political ideologies like Nazism and Communism were so sure they were right that they have sacrificed the lives of millions who did not agree or who were not the right sort of people, in the gas chambers of Germany, the gulags of Russia and the killing fields of Cambodia. 'Perhaps', say some people, 'the very idea of having the truth is the root of all this.'

- Individual people find that there is a spiritual vacuum in them which no amount of science or technology or material possessions can satisfy. The way to happiness promised by the Enlightenment, namely material prosperity and control over nature has not produced happiness. Jesus said, 'What will it profit a man if he gains the whole world, and loses his own soul?' (Mark 8:36, NKJV). Many Westerners today are depressed people. For all their wealth and labour-saving gadgets, quality of life eludes them. It does not seem to be something which mere reason and technology can provide.

- Presented with so many choices, life has become so complex for many people that they have given up on their reasoning powers and prefer to live by their feelings. They choose what seems to feel good. That's an easier thing to decide. Very often people feel that this gives them a more exciting and 'authentic' existence than the safe choices of 'rationality'. Many a person has said to themselves, for example, 'I know cannabis may harm me, but who cares! It makes me feel good.' Once again, reason is set aside. They go with their instincts.

- TV and the internet, which continue to be overwhelmingly dominant in our media, now present no commonly agreed view of life, but rather a welter of entertaining images which lack moral or intellectual cohesion. Within one TV news programme you might be presented with the sincerely held views of secularists, Muslims, the gay community, Buddhists etc. Who is to say who is right? This also adds to the acceptability of the post-modern outlook.

These are some of the ways in which the 'unreasonable' post-modern mentality has begun to take root in Western culture. As Christians, we are once again reminded of Paul's words in Romans 1. To discard our God-given ability to reason is obvious foolishness. But that is where we end up when we set God aside. While rejoicing in the salvation which comes through the cross of Christ, the apostle Paul reiterates the darkness of the unconverted human mind, 'Has not God made foolish the wisdom of the world?' (1 Cor. 1:20).

The product of sin

And there is more to it. Our ignorance is not simply a product of the fact that we are finite, small creatures with limited minds. According to the Bible, we are a fallen race. The human heart has become sinful, corrupt and self-centred. It wants to run its own show with no interference from God (or, indeed, anyone else). An incoherent world-view (like that of post-modernism) inevitably produces a world without clear moral values, and this leaves the individual totally free to choose for himself/herself how to live. Under the influence of a fallen human nature, this can only go in one direction. 'They are darkened in their understanding and separated from the life of God because of the ignorance that is in them due to the hardening of their hearts. Having lost all sensitivity, they have given themselves over to sensuality so as to indulge in every kind of impurity, with a continual lust for more' (Eph. 4:18-19). It doesn't tend towards reason but towards a fallen 'feel good'.

Although no one can actually live daily life without believing in some kind of objective truth and reliable communication, PM turns us in upon ourselves. The only 'truth' that has any validity is 'what is true for you'. Thus we have entered a 'sinner's paradise'. If the logic of PM is followed to its destination, then we reach a philosophy of life where people can feel completely unrestrained. They and they alone set the agenda. The dominance of human nature by sin lies behind the emergence of post-modernism too.

How is PM affecting us?

Many of the trends which we see developing in contemporary society originate in the post-modern outlook. Here is a selection, and among them you will find political correctness.

- *The death of thought.* This follows from there being no truth. 'The fact is that debate and rational argument no longer have a central place in the world of the young, and not only because the sound-bite culture has pushed them aside. Children are taught from an early age not to judge between opinions – to be 'sensitive' towards other cultures and other ways of thinking. If all options are equally valid, then none of them really matters – such is the inevitable conclusion of the multicultural and inclusive curriculum' (Professor Roger Scruton, *The Sunday Times,* 1 August 1999). This is how political correctness feeds back into post-modernism.

- *Demise of church and community.* If there is no truth, and words mean nothing, then there is nothing on which to base community, to bring people together. In recent decades we have seen the demise of the traditional institutions which have served the community. If there is no common truth, then there is no common good. So why join a political party? Why go to church if your opinion is just as valid as that of the Bible? The new 'cyber-communities' which have emerged from things like being 'friends' on Facebook have no real common purpose except that of the individual broadcasting his/her life to a select group who may be interested. Although it seems to be a community it is more about individualism – even, some may say, narcissism.

- *The inadmissibility of criticising groups other than your own.* This is the heart of political correctness. If there is no truth, then all religious, political, and ethical outlooks are equally valid. It is simply out of place, for example, to criticise anyone else's religion or sexual orientation. Because you are not part of that religious or sexual culture you cannot possibly understand it. Truth is an insider thing. There are no universals by which outsiders can critique others. So keep quiet. How can you possibly criticise it? What you say might be hurtful. And what gives you the right to hurt or offend others? The arch-heresy is to argue that your outlook is right for everyone – as if there was a God who knows what is best for everyone. Truth is simply a power play which has been used to oppress others. Therefore we should not care about so-called 'facts': we should simply be on the side of those we see as victims of the system. PC draws on this way of thinking.

- *Suspicion of all authority.* If there is no truth which is true for all, then all government, even that which purports to be democratic and for our common 'good', is invalid. Why should the majority decide what is 'good' for me? Teachers and parents are challenged as to whether they have the right to correct children. Doctors are in two minds as to whether they have the right to prescribe for patients or save their lives. Perhaps they do not want to be saved. Rejection of morality, law and order follows. Wasn't there something of this driving the rioting and looting in many cities in the UK in the summer of 2011?

It makes one wonder whether in future it will be accepted that disputes should be settled by power rather than by argument or justice. PM could easily lead us back to the law of the jungle.

- *Victim culture.* With no truth by which to arbitrate, post-modernism fosters the view that the powerful are always in the wrong. So many factions in society now make headway by seeking to prove that 'I am more victimised than you.' Words like 'Islamophobia' and 'homophobia' have come to the fore. Everyone wants to be portrayed as someone who has been hard done by. This is the result of post-modernism and political correctness.

- *Therapy culture.* We will say more about this later. But beginning in the 1980s, the idea of caring for others has plugged into the idea of boosting a person's self-esteem or self-worth, with little or no reference to what is right or wrong. This fits entirely with relativism and the PM outlook. If there is no God and no overarching meaning to the world, then people and how they feel about themselves must become the greatest priority. Some would say that this therapy approach to life (making people feel good about themselves) has even undermined the validity of our school examination system. *All Must Have Prizes* is a well-known book by Melanie Phillips examining this phenomenon. And for many years at the beginning of the 21st century we saw the numbers of those getting top grades at A-level climbing higher each year. Apparently young people were becoming more and more clever? A teacher's first concern, it seems, is not to teach and to test, but to make his or her pupils feel good about themselves. This same approach led to competitive sports being frowned upon in many schools.

- *Consumer culture.* The heart of consumerism is personal choice and individual self-expression. We do not simply want to buy necessary items. We want to buy items which say who we are. Our shopping shows our personality. Clothing and other items are to be seen more as accessories. This same thinking has broken out of the shopping mall into wider areas of life. The NHS, Government, and more seek to give choice. But there is a problem with this. It leads to a lack of 'joined-up thinking' in our society and our services, as different people's choices may require contradictory measures. This leads to inefficiency and muddle.

- *Love of conspiracy theories.* The idea that all claims to truth are power plays means that every claim to truth is a conspiracy. With this mindset, TV programmes like *The X-Files* (government conspiracy) and novels like *The Da Vinci Code* (church conspiracy) commend themselves to PM people. They give the message, 'You are right to suspect everything!'

- *The virtue of disbelief.* According to PM, any truth claim is not only not true, it is actually a power play. So all truth claims must be debunked − or deconstructed. This will insulate you from falling into the clutches of 'their' power play. Disbelief is, therefore, the only safe choice. This is very different from the Enlightenment, rationalistic virtue of 'keeping an open mind'. Now there is seen to be a virtue in having a 'closed mind'. And so we are back where we started this list, with the death of thought.

Many of the items on this list conspire together to make Christian evangelism particularly difficult today. It is an outlook which hardens people's hearts so that they will not even listen to the gospel. Taken to its logical conclusion, it is not too far-fetched to say that PM actually threatens freedom of speech and therefore the very survival of Western civilization.

How are we to respond to PM?

First of all, the Christian should not be discouraged. God is still sovereign, and the fact that in PM human philosophy has said or is in the process of saying 'goodbye' to rationality in many areas, only proves its emptiness (Rom. 1:21-22).

It is the fear of the LORD which is the beginning of wisdom (Prov. 9:10). The way society is disintegrating into decadence and foolishness through having ignored God only serves to prove the Christian position. That actually gives us more reason to think that our faith is true; that our God is there. In that we can take great comfort.

Second, we are to see the same thing from the positive angle. We are to see that only Christianity provides the proper meta-narrative. It gives us the overarching story which makes sense of the world and is liveable. Truth is guaranteed by God. The Scriptures are God's word, are reliable, and ground us in absolute truth. This is not simply a random leap of faith. We find that as we believe God's truth it makes sense of what we see around us in the world and life becomes liveable. Jesus said, 'Heaven and earth will pass away, but my words will never pass away' (Luke 21:33). We are to unashamedly live and preach the Bible story and its truth.

Third, the truth of Christ must be shared with practical Christian love to this very lost and increasingly hardened generation. People will not be convinced by a theoretical argument, but by changed lives, truth lived, enjoyed and applied. 'In the same way, let your light shine before men, that they may see your good deeds and praise your Father in heaven' (Matt. 5:16). Our culture may have changed, but, hallelujah, our God has not! 'Jesus Christ is the same yesterday and today and forever' (Heb. 13:8).

Recommended reading:

Douglas Coupland, *Generation X: Tales for an Accelerated Culture* (New York: St Martin's Press, 1991).
Os Guinness, *Time for Truth* (Leicester: IVP, 2000)
Erroll Hulse, *Postmodernism* (Pensacola: Chapel Library, 2007)
D. A. Carson, *The Gagging of God* (Leicester: Apollos/IVP, 1996)
D. A. Carson, *Becoming Conversant with the Emerging Church* (Grand Rapids: Zondervan, 2005)

Chapter 3
What is political correctness?

Some years ago the European Monitoring Centre on Racism and Xenophobia commissioned a report on anti-Semitism (offences targeting Jewish people) in Europe.

But when the report was given to them they suppressed it as it had found that the main cause of rising anti-Jewish violence in Europe was Muslim youths; not white skinheads and neo-fascists, as they had expected. The authors of the report, who were Jewish, were told to rewrite it because, as it stood, it would undermine the EMCR's work helping Muslims and pro-Palestinian groups. When the authors protested that that was opposite to the evidence, the EMCR rewrote the report itself and published a conclusion which was totally at odds with the research. All this was reported in the *Daily Telegraph* on 23 November 2003.

In our contemporary world, political correctness frequently trumps factual correctness. So, for example, on the issue of women's pay being less on average than men's the PC people will tell us that this is due to sexual discrimination. While there may be some truth in that, it seems that actually it has more to do with women's different life choices; including decisions to have children and look after them, and so take time out of work and away from the work-place. This leads to their total earnings being less than those of men. But it is not politically correct to say that. Similar examples could be multiplied. We live in a PC world. We need to understand it.

Concern for justice

What is political correctness? It is a difficult beast to pin down. My best shot at defining PC succinctly would be something like the following: 'Political correctness is a way of thinking that classifies certain groups of people as victims of society who should be treated differently from other people in order to correct perceived injustices and to shield them from being offended.'

In many ways, of course, this can be seen as an admirable aim. Where people are real victims who have suffered true injustice we ought to be seeking to do something to put things right. The living God who has revealed himself in Christ is a God of justice (Deut. 32:4).

But it is at this point that the shift in our society towards atheism comes into play. As we have seen, without God (or at least an agreed meta-narrative for our civilization), there can be no agreed moral framework. This is what post-modernism insists upon. But without a moral framework the whole concept of justice, what is right and fair, is up for grabs. It is malleable. It is seen in different ways by different people. This means that concern about treating people 'fairly' becomes a foggy area. The concept of 'fairness' becomes open to manipulation. In particular, in seeking to 'protect' those it deems as victims, PC is quite willing to treat others unfairly as part of its process.

In his book *What's Left?* investigating the demise of old-fashioned left-wing politics in Britain, the journalist Nick

Cohen says this about the collapse of socialism in the 1980s under the onslaught of the thinking and success of British Prime Minister Margaret Thatcher and US President Ronald Reagan:

> But as many radical intellectuals in the West retreated into the lecture halls before the tide of conservatism… they fled from universal values. To generalize, the idea that a homosexual black woman should have the same rights as a heterosexual white man was replaced by a relativism which took the original hopeful challenge of the early feminist, gay and anti-racial movements and flipped it over. Homosexuality, blackness and womanhood became separate cultures that couldn't be criticized or understood by outsiders applying universal criteria. Nor, by extension, could any other culture, even if it was the culture of fascism, religious tyranny, wife burning or suicide bombing.

He is highlighting the distortion of justice. He is describing the emergence of political correctness.

Obviously, as Christians, we should be encouraging consideration for the more vulnerable members of our society. But should we be doing that in a way which ignores what is just for others? In its early days, back in the 1980s, political correctness no doubt had good intentions. But as its influence has grown, two things have happened.

First, as indicated by Nick Cohen, such protection of the potential victims of society has got to the point where frequently truth is ignored or suppressed under cover of the post-modern outlook which tells us that no one can understand any group to which they do not belong. Accepting this means that it is impossible to speak of justice in the traditional way of a fairness which applies to everyone.

Second, bizarrely, although based on an outlook which insists that there are no moral absolutes, many advocates of political correctness have used their stance to take the moral high ground and conduct witch-hunts against those who do not see things their way.

Equality?

So what has gone wrong here? It all comes down to a misunderstanding, manipulation or misuse of one word – equality.

We have become accustomed to thinking that where there is equality there is justice. And, yes, that common sense position does take us in the right direction, generally speaking. We are all familiar with this. For example, at the family meal table, two siblings feel a sense of injustice if Mum does not dole out the pudding correctly. 'He's got more than me. It's not fair!' And, rightly, Mum will do her best to equalise the portions.

But this broad concept of equality has to be thought through a little more carefully. It is a word which appears simple but actually is quite complex. For a start, there are different areas of equality. There might be equality in one area, while not in another.

This is obvious from everyday life. For example, a tennis ball and a cricket ball may be more or less equal in size, but they are quite different in weight – and if one is going to get hit on the head by one of them, I know which one I would choose. Again, five £1 coins are equal in value to a £5 note; but in other ways they are not equal at all. One can be set on fire with a match, for example, while the other cannot.

Equal as citizens

In the same way, there are different areas of equality which need to be considered when we consider human society. Traditionally, a just and fair society is characterised by equality for all its citizens in three overlapping areas:

- *First*, there is what I might call an *existential* equality. That is that every individual equally has the right to exist and should have access to means of sustaining their life. Biblically, this equality is enshrined in God's command, 'You shall not murder' (Exod. 20:13). Historically, sadly, this has not always been accepted, leading to genocides and holocausts (Exod. 1:22). But where there is existential equality, it means (for example) not only that every citizen has the right to life, but also every able-bodied person has an equal right to seek work and provide for themselves and their families. No one is to be barred from appropriate employment on the basis of their creed or colour or gender or (generally) anything else. Where, through a national economic downturn or through personal disability, etc., employment opportunities are less than are required, a civilized society will provide some form of safety-net of support which again is open equally to all. In ancient Israel, the edges of the fields were left unharvested, so that the poor might have food if they gathered it (Lev. 19:9-10). In modern Britain we have a welfare state which is highly commendable in many ways, though it is open to abuse from people who do not wish to work for a living.

- *Second*, there is *legal* equality. This is the idea that everyone, from the greatest to the least in the land, should be subject to the same laws. There should not be one set of rules for one group in society and a different set of laws for others. There should not be one law for the rich and another for the poor. There should not be one set of rules for the king and a different set of rules for commoners. The concept of a constitutional monarchy where the king does not make the rules but is subject to the laws of the land finds its origins in the Bible. Moses instructed that when someone became king in Israel, he was to copy out the laws which God had given as a reminder that it was under these laws that he was to govern and that he himself was answerable to these laws (Deut.17: 18-19).

- *Third*, there is *political* equality. This is the principle that, in a democracy, every adult should be able to participate in the democratic process. It is the idea that, rich or poor, male or female, religious or non-religious, old or young (within the agreed boundaries of adulthood), everyone has a vote of equal value and we are all free to stand for election to government should we so wish. The roots of political equality go back to Biblical truths concerning the equality of all human beings before God. We are all made in God's image (Gen. 1:26-27). So, for example, the Lollard preacher, John Ball, who was prominent in the Peasant's Revolt of 1381 which sought to assert the rights of the common people, was famous for his sermon in which he asked the rhetorical question, 'When Adam delved and Eve span, who was then the gentleman?'

Together these three equalities, based on Biblical values, led the Western world in the direction of the great freedoms which we have held so precious – freedom of conscience, freedom of speech, freedom of assembly and freedom of the press.

Having thought about the general areas of equality in a civilized society, we now need to think a little more deeply.

Different categories of equality

As we consider the subject of equality and the kind of language used by PC organisations and spokespersons, we come to realise that beneath the rhetoric different categories of equality are being referred to.

Going back to the analogies we used earlier we might say that when we compare the volumes and the weights of cricket balls and tennis balls we are talking about physical equalities. But when we think about five £1 coins and compare them with a £5 note, though they are not equal at all physically, yet financially they are equal. Here the physical and the financial are two different categories of equality.

In considering human society, there are different categories of equality. We can think of these in terms of what we might call the three 'o's. These are equality of outset, equality of opportunity, and equality of outcome.

Equality of outset
An athletics race is only considered fair if all the contestants start at the same time from the same place, at the same distance from the finishing line. In life, of course, we do not all start at the same place. It is to be hoped that when we are

born into the world we are all seen as having an equal right to be here. Nevertheless, there can still be major differences; some are born healthy and well, while others are sadly born with congenital illnesses; some are born into poverty, others into riches, etc. But even if a pair of identical twins are born into the same family, that does not guarantee that their lives will turn out the same. One thinks of the classic (though not identical) twins in Scripture, Jacob and Esau (Gen. 25:24). They shared the same mother and father, but made different choices in life and went in very different directions. Equality of outset is not something we can bring about. In order to do anything like it we would need to enter the realms of science-fiction eugenics and produce a population in which every person was a clone of every other. That is not achievable; and many of us would say that it is not desirable. Society at large benefits from different people having different gifts used for the benefit of the whole (1 Cor. 12:7). Nevertheless, going back to our analogy of a race only being fair if all the runners start at the same point, we can see that the idea of seeking to give every child a good start in life is a good aim.

Equality of opportunity
This is the principle that holds that everyone should be in a position to achieve the best they can in life, given their talents and willingness to work hard. It is the foundation of the ideal of a 'meritocracy'. In general, we approve of an open society in which bright, hard-working individuals can achieve their potential and rise to the top of the pile. Jesus' parable of the sower (Mark 4:1–8) is an example of equal opportunity. There were different kinds of ground: the path, the rocky soil, the soil already occupied by thorns, and the good soil. They were all treated in the same way. All the different kinds of ground had the good seed scattered on them. But once again, though

they were all treated alike, that did not guarantee that they all produced a crop.

Equality of outcome

This is where everyone ends up in the same place. It is where everyone finishes with more or less the same wealth and the same 'position' in society. This was the kind of dream which initially drove Communism, so much associated with Karl Marx and Frederich Engels. There would be a pooling of resources, and people would all be given the same out of the collective pot, or at least take out only what they needed. Going back to our illustration of life as an athletics race, equality of outcome insists that no matter where people start or how great an effort they make, everyone ought to break the finishing tape together. When it is put like that, we feel how inherently unfair this type of equality can be.

Interestingly, Jesus told another parable which is an example of equality of outcome. This is the parable of the workers in the vineyard (Matt. 20:1-16). Labourers were taken on by the master of the vineyard at different times during the day and worked until evening. When it came to paying them their wages, he gave each of them what they had agreed with him to work for. Unbeknown to each other, they had all agreed on the same wage for the day, so they were all paid the same. This led those who had worked longest to feel hard done by. But the master replied that each of them had agreed, and it was down to him to give to each of them as he had decided. This equality of outcome parable is not meant to teach us about scales of pay for industry or the management of society. It is actually a parable about God's grace. It is teaching that salvation is not by works. It is all of God's free kindness, regardless of our deserving. And people can be saved right up to the last moment of their lives quite apart from how much of their lives might be left in which to serve him. In one sense this equality of outcome might look 'unfair'; but that is the nature of God's free grace.

Looking at these three different categories of equality, equality of outset, of opportunity, and of outcome, we can begin to make some broad points about the change which is happening in our society and the emergence of political correctness.

Traditional 'fairness'

Generally speaking, old-fashioned 'fairness' comes under the category of equality of opportunity. This begins with existential equality, the right to life and sustenance. (Obviously, the abortion issue is sadly an attack on this, but that subject is outside the scope of this book). At a practical level, not everyone can have the same start in life, but a civilized society makes some attempt to do what it can to give children a good start. Thus we have free medical care, free schooling and even free school meals for those who are in great poverty. Then, moving into responsible adulthood, we have legal and political equality. Ideally we believe that everyone should have the same opportunity to be defended at law when that is required, and that everyone should have the same opportunity to participate in the democratic process.

In colloquial language it is about giving everyone 'a fair chance' in life.

Further, it needs to be said that this equality of opportunity which we have in mind when we think in traditional terms of what is 'fair' is wedded to a moral framework. For example, though all have access to the law, we believe that for someone to try to bribe the police or the judge is a misuse of the system which breaks the rules of fairness. Neither do we believe that one child should be given a place at a certain school solely because they come from a middle-class Anglo-Saxon family, while another child should be denied a place solely because his or her background is that of a poor ethnic minority. In a school system which is meant to be equally open to all, this would not be fair. (If parents want to spend their money on sending their children to private schools, that is a different matter). Similarly, if a student gained a place at a good university but later it was found that they had lied about the exam results required for entrance, then we would feel that they had breached the rules and should be dismissed. It is those who have honestly worked hard and obtained the grades legitimately who should be awarded the places.

Traditional fairness, then, would say that we try to give everyone, as far as possible, equal opportunities; but what they make of those opportunities is up to them. There is a responsibility on the individual. We all have to work hard and make the best of what we have. Traditionally, we have understood that this world is not always fair. (Here the Christian view that we live in a fallen world underlies much common thinking.) Accidents and wars and illnesses and all kinds of things may thwart our desired path in life; but we must all do our best to make the most of our opportunities.

Political correctness

But when we move into the thinking of political correctness, things begin to change. *Firstly*, of course, political correctness does embrace the idea of equality of opportunity. Minority groups should not have less access to education or welfare or the law or the democratic process than others.

However, *secondly,* political correctness would also want to embrace equality of outcome as part of what is necessary in a fair society. It would say that unless we all end up in basically the same place in life, something is wrong; the system is unfair. The outcome should be the same, regardless of the choices we have made in life. This outlook tends to shift responsibility away from the individual and load it onto 'the system'.

Let us go back for a moment to something we said at the beginning of the chapter. We raised the issue of women's pay. On average, women's pay tends to be less than men's. But, while there may be some bad employers who still find ways to pay women less (and I do not want to defend them), a major factor behind this situation, as we noted earlier, is the fact that many women choose to leave work, sometimes for long periods of time, in order to have children and look after them. There is nothing wrong with that. That is wonderful. But to think that, having made that choice, somehow they should still end up with the same pay as a man who has not left work (or indeed another woman who has decided not to have children) is unfair. We all make choices in life, and it is only right that we accept the consequences of our choices. In a traditional way of thinking, we would say that you can't have your cake and eat it. But PC argues, why shouldn't they have their cake and eat it too?

Another example of political correctness insisting on equality of outcome is the drive to give children to homosexual couples who want them. Much research indicates that statistically children thrive best where there is both a mother and a father. But even what is likely to be best for the child is set aside in order to manufacture an equality of outcome. The fact that people have chosen a way of life which makes the having of children naturally an impossibility is set aside. Hence lesbians should have IVF treatment and gay men should be allowed to adopt. Equality of outcome, namely a family with children, is required regardless of all else.

So we can see how the differences between traditional fairness and political correctness begin to open up.

Equal percentages everywhere?

Let us pick up again on the matter of education. The politically correct would look at the percentages of different groups within the general population and then, wedded to this equality of outcome view of equality, make the assumption that unless those same percentages are present in (say) the student population of the top universities or the people sitting on the boards of our top companies, then there must have been some great injustice at work. That may be the case, but it may well not be. The truth is that given the same opportunities some people are simply more gifted than others and some people are simply prepared to work harder than others. Indeed, some ethnic groups have a reputation for being particularly hard workers, while others do not.

But going further, political correctness would say in this case that something must be done in order to guarantee the percentages in the population being reflected in, say, the top universities. Candidates from under-represented backgrounds must be given preferential treatment over those from well-represented backgrounds. This is 'right' because the under-represented group are seen as victims. It is called 'positive discrimination'. But what that means is injustice in the old-fashioned sense. It will mean that, because there are only a certain number of undergraduate places, a more able student from a well-represented group will miss out on a place in order to make way for a less able student from an under-represented background. Whereas, previously, university entrance was blind to different backgrounds, and it was all down to exam results, now it is no longer simply dependent on exam performance.

This willingness to promote injustice (in traditional terms) in order to positively promote those the politically correct have identified as victims can then easily lead on to a distortion of the truth. As was explained at the beginning of the chapter, the fact that the rise in anti-semitism in Europe was actually down to some Muslims (a 'victim' group), rather than people from the white majority (who are not a 'victim' group), meant that the authors of the 2003 report were told to rewrite it.

In the hands of the more aggressive proponents of PC, also influenced by post-modernism's denial of absolute truth, the concern for those they see as victims leads to an almost total abandonment of rational argument. We fall quickly into the politics of intimidation and shouting down opponents. After all, if there is no such thing as truth, and all truth claims are merely power plays in order to manipulate others, then the logic leads to the abandonment of debate and reliance instead upon threats.

Though, no doubt, there were good intentions behind the origins of political correctness, we have begun to see how it causes difficulties, especially in its push towards bringing about equal outcomes for all rather than the traditional concern with equal opportunities.

God's grace

Someone reading this chapter might ask, 'If, in the parable of the workers, God gives equal outcomes, what can be so wrong with us trying to bring about equal outcomes for all people?' If equal outcome is the product of God's grace, then shouldn't we follow God's pattern?

There are three things to say briefly in answer to that objection.

First, unlike (for example) university places, there is no limit on places in God's kingdom. His freely including in his forgiveness those who ask for it in no way means that his forgiveness is less available to others.

Second, the politically correct wish to see equal outcomes for everyone no matter what their life choices. They desire an unquestioned universalism. By contrast, God places responsibility on us as individuals. Yes, the grace of God is there for all in Jesus Christ. But we must choose Christ. If we do not, then we must live with the consequences.

Third, politically correct concern for equality of outcome has emerged out of a background of post-modernism which denies the existence of absolute moral values. Political correctness does its best to be amoral in the traditional sense. But the free grace of God does not set aside moral issues. Rather, it recognizes the seriousness of sin, but deals with our moral failures through the cross of Christ, where he paid the penalty for our sins on our behalf.

So, although God's grace does bring about the equal outcome of salvation for believing sinners, it does not do so in any unjust way. God's grace does not set aside traditional justice, but rather upholds it (Rom. 3:31).

God's concern for minorities

If political correctness mishandles concern for minorities or the vulnerable in society in a way which breaches justice, what is the right way to approach the issue? One way of understanding the Bible's answer is by turning to Exodus 22:21 – 23:9.

> [21]Do not mistreat an alien or oppress him, for you were aliens in Egypt. [22]Do not take advantage of a widow or an orphan. [23]If you do and they cry out to me, I will certainly hear their cry. [24]My anger will be aroused, and I will kill you with the sword; your wives will become widows and your children fatherless. [25]If you lend money to one of my people among you who is needy, do not be like a moneylender; charge him no interest. [26] If you take your neighbour's cloak as a pledge, return it to him by sunset, [27]because his cloak is the only covering he has for his body. What else will he sleep in? When he cries out to me, I will hear, for I am compassionate. [28]Do not blaspheme God or curse the ruler of your people.
>
> [29]Do not hold back offerings from your granaries or your vats. You must give me the firstborn of your sons.

³⁰Do the same with your cattle and your sheep. Let them stay with their mothers for seven days, but give them to me on the eighth day. ³¹You are to be my holy people. So do not eat the meat of an animal torn by wild beasts; throw it to the dogs.

¹Do not spread false reports. Do not help a wicked man by being a malicious witness. ²Do not follow the crowd in doing wrong. When you give testimony in a lawsuit, do not pervert justice by siding with the crowd, ³and do not show favouritism to a poor man in his lawsuit. ⁴If you come across your enemy's ox or donkey wandering off, be sure to take it back to him. ⁵If you see the donkey of someone who hates you fallen down under its load, do not leave it there; be sure you help him with it. ⁶Do not deny justice to your poor people in their lawsuits. ⁷Have nothing to do with a false charge and do not put an innocent or honest person to death, for I will not acquit the guilty. ⁸Do not accept a bribe, for a bribe blinds those who see and twists the words of the righteous. ⁹Do not oppress an alien; you yourselves know how it feels to be aliens, because you were aliens in Egypt.

We can see that this portion of Scripture is meant to be taken as a unit, by comparing 22:21 and 23:9, the top and tail of the section. Both remind Israel of their own time in Egypt and command God's people not to oppress an alien, a foreigner.

Here we have some of the commands of God for Old Testament Israel. You see that the verses split quite neatly into three parts.

First, in 22:21-28 we are given teaching about care for the disadvantaged and people who might be different from us. Do not mistreat or oppress a foreigner... Do not take advantage of a widow or an orphan....Do not charge interest on an emergency loan... Do not revile or curse rulers (22:21, 22, 25, 28). We might not see rulers as different from us, but of course they are perceived as an 'elite'. So here we are dealing with people who are different from the ordinary person in Israel because of race, or poverty, or higher social status. Notice that God's concern here is for an equality of treatment. They are not to be ill-treated or taken advantage of or reviled. Putting that positively, in contemporary terms we would say they are to be given equal opportunity.

Second, in 22:29-31 Israel is reminded of various duties towards their holy God. Israel is told not to do certain things on the basis that they belong to God. 'You are to be my holy people' (22:31).

Then *thirdly*, in 23:1-9 there is teaching about care for truthfulness and what is right. 'Do not spread false reports. Do not help a wicked man by being a malicious witness. Do not follow the crowd in doing wrong. When you give testimony in a lawsuit, do not pervert justice by siding with the crowd, and do not show favouritism to a poor man in his lawsuit' (23:1-3). Here the Israelites are to be committed to truth no matter what other influences may impinge upon them. They are not even to let the fact that some 'enemy' had mistreated them in the past affect their commitment to doing only what is right and true.

Balancing the seesaw

Imagine a seesaw. Think of the central verses about duties to God as the pivot in the middle. On one side of the pivot is concern for the disadvantaged, while on the other is concern for truth. The seesaw is balanced between care for the disadvantaged and care for truth. There is balance.

But as we saw in our first two chapters, when we looked at the consequences of atheism and the rise of post-modernism, if you remove God, then inevitably truth and morality lose any objective reality and become whatever you want to make them. That means two things.

First, going back to our seesaw analogy, you no longer have to care for the truth and morality side, and the seesaw tips over totally on the side of the 'disadvantaged'. This is PC. According to political correctness, all are not equal before the law. Those deemed to be disadvantaged have special status for the reasons we have explained earlier.

Second, having got rid of the truth and morality side of the seesaw, we move away from reasoned argument. This usually leaves us to be guided by emotion. We will favour the poor man in the lawsuit – even if he is a thief and a liar. He is poor. That is all that matters. Therefore we must be on his side. Political correctness plays on things like guilt feelings or sympathy, not truth. We may feel guilty that we ourselves have more money than the poor man. He may indeed arouse our sympathy when we think of his circumstances. But actually these things have no bearing on whether or not he committed the crime. Experience tells us that a poor man can be an embezzler just as much as a rich man.

Notice that in taking the stance it does, PC tends to be extremely patronizing. The poor man is a victim. It could not possibly be that he is a free agent who has made his own decisions and is prepared to take responsibility for where his choices have led him. Of course, some poor people are victims of circumstances. But many are not. They have ended up where they are because of decisions for which they are responsible. So political correctness tends to categorize certain groups of people as victims; then, having done that, it is not so much interested in truth as simply being pro-victim. But as far as God is concerned, truth is just as important as compassion.

We can see, then, that though there may be good intentions behind PC it is very different from God's command to Israel.

Recommended reading:

Peter Saunders, *The Rise of the Equalities Industry* (London: Civitas, 2011)

Chapter 4
Some results of political correctness

How is PC changing Western society? What are the consequences of this PC way of seeing things becoming so prevalent?

Political correctness is closing down freedom in many areas. The great upward path of Western society to produce a society in which, within the rule of law, individuals enjoy liberty of thought and of expression is being put into reverse.

In his book, *The Liberal Delusion,* John Marsh puts this very clearly, speaking of the relationship between 'equality' and freedom as a zero-sum game because freedom and equality must inevitably run into conflict with each other. He writes:

> There is a trade-off between freedom and equality. If we are given freedom, then because we have different amounts of intelligence, talent and luck, we will end up unequal over time. Friedrich Hayek held that human beings are not born equal and if we treat them equally the outcome will be inequality. So paradoxically equality can only be achieved by treating people unequally. There are different answers to this fundamental conflict, but all solutions involve different trade-offs between freedom and equality, which remains a zero-sum game: the more

freedom the less equality; and the more equality the less freedom.

We are beginning to see this bite with the loss of freedom (especially, it seems, for Christians) in the Western world. Freedom of speech is under attack. Pastor Ake Green was sentenced to prison in Sweden in 2003 for expressing the fact that the Bible teaches that homosexual practice is a sin. Two pastors faced prison in Australia for expressing their disagreement with the teachings of Islam in 2004. In Britain a teacher was sacked from her job in 2009 simply for asking a pupil if they would like her to pray for them. These cases can be multiplied. People are no longer free to express things as they were in previous years. Even legitimate public debate or showing care to others may be deemed illegitimate. Freedom is being taken away.

Another of the most worrying results of political correctness is its propensity to bring the law into disrepute. Traditionally, the laws of the land give expression to social norms for which all its citizens have a respect. To take a trivial example, throughout society there would be an agreement that it is sensible for the speed limit through the middle of a busy high street to be 30 mph. There may be those who might wish to see it lowered to 20 mph, and there might be a fair argument for that. But to allow it to be raised to 70 mph would bring an understandable outcry. We prohibit such things as stealing, assault and fraud because almost everyone would acknowledge that such acts are wrong and that those who engage in them pose a threat to the entire community.

However, the areas in which political correctness has intervened tend to command much less support from the general public. As I have mentioned before, there have even been examples where, for example, ostensibly for PC reasons local councils have barred the display of Christmas decorations in town centres during December. It was said that such actions were taken in order not to offend people who belong to religions other than Christianity. But when people of other religions were asked whether they were offended by a display of angels and shepherds and Christmas lights, they said no; actually, they quite liked them. All this smacks not of laws evolving by common consent from within the community, but of dictats being imposed from above by a powerful elite made up of PC people who feel that they know better than everybody else, including those they pretend to be protecting.

Every time this happens, respect for the law and the legislative process among the general public is eroded a little further.

More consequences

There are many other consequences of the rise of PC in our society. They are probably too many to enumerate. We can only pick up on a few things. I state them starkly.

The destruction of justice

Although our society has been bamboozled into thinking that treating people equally means treating people justly, sometimes it does not. Sometimes it is very unjust to treat people equally.

Here is a pertinent example. From Friday 21 December 2012, women in Britain had to pay the same car insurance premiums as men, despite the fact that on average women have far fewer accidents and are much safer drivers than men. This is a ruling from the European Court of Justice which is unjust, because it is treating men and women drivers as equals when they are not. Because people are not the same, often it is unjust to treat them as if they are.

Although advocates of PC would say that they are fighting for justice and that their aim is a redistribution of power, immediately we see that where political correctness pertains, society runs in a totally different way from that which we have traditionally known. Vindication and support are not about who is right and who is wrong in the old-fashioned sense. Neither are they about who is telling the truth and who is not. They tend to be about obtaining victim status. If you can sustain a claim that 'I am more victimised that you', you are likely to get the verdict. So, to take an obvious example, America (as the world's most powerful country) can never do any good in the eyes of the politically correct. Even though it is the largest donor of overseas aid and has done more than any other country to spread liberal democracy, defeating both Nazism and Communism, it is continually attacked by the PC media. Doubtless, America is far from perfect; but this shows prejudice rather than fairness. God says, 'Acquitting the guilty and condemning the innocent – the LORD detests them both' (Prov. 17:15).

The destruction of debate

Politically incorrect arguments are simply dismissed and not engaged with. During the debate concerning the redefinition of marriage in 2012, the Coalition for Marriage organised a petition calling for traditional heterosexual marriage to be retained. They collected well over half a million signatures. The petition was handed in at Downing Street by a married couple, Rhys and Esther Curnow, dressed in formal wedding clothes. They immediately became the targets of intense 'cyber-bullying'. They received over a hundred hate messages, including threats of violence and death, to their publicly available Facebook pages. No one from the gay lobby seemed interested in engaging the argument. There was no debate in the messages, simply threats.

Many people who have embraced PC see their opponents as not just wrong but bad, and therefore they feel free to resort to personal attacks on them. But God says, 'The first to present his case seems right, till another comes forward and questions him' (Prov. 18:17). We are called to reason and to listen to both sides of an argument. This is being lost.

The destruction of tolerance
Liberal democracy, which still (just about) rules in the West, has historically been quite happy for people to hold different opinions. There is freedom of speech so long as people do not stir up or promote violence. The scientific community does not bother to try to send people to jail for believing that the moon is made of green cheese or that the earth is flat. It simply believes that reason will prove them wrong. By and large, it is happy to shrug its shoulders and let reality show itself over time. Although not without its faults and darker moments, generally speaking Protestant Christianity has fostered freedom of speech and given birth to democracy.

But PC allows no dissent. With the abandonment of reason in political correctness there has arisen an intolerance of other people's positions. PC appears to wish to legislate for what people are and are not allowed to think. Having set out to promote a more tolerant society, in supporting those it sees as victims it has ended by becoming a vehicle for great intolerance, especially towards religious people.

The self-hatred of the West

Because political correctness champions those perceived as victims, and because for the last three or four hundred years the West has dominated the globe, and been generally prosperous and healthy and powerful, Westerners are somehow made to feel guilty about this. We must have obtained this power illegitimately. This self-hatred was particularly seen in the way events in the aftermath of the Iraq war were reported. Although the coalition forces were there seeking to bring peace, freedom, prosperity and democracy, and it was the insurgents who were causing all the deaths with their suicide bombs – somehow news agencies like the politically-correct BBC managed continually to report events in such a way that often the impression was given that Western soldiers were setting out to kill innocent people every day.

The disenfranchising of the church

Since the PC world is on the side of those it perceives as victims, the church has lost status and credibility. This often seems strange to Christians. 'Why is preference given to not offending Muslims or Hindus, but no one seems to care about offending the Christians?' we ask. It seems unjust; and in traditional, common sense terms, it is unjust.

The reason in PC terms is probably to do with the fact that in the past the West has been composed of 'Christian' countries. There have been state churches across Europe. The church and the government have worked hand in hand. For example, The Church of England is headed by the Queen. There are still Anglican bishops in the House of Lords. Thus the church (and sadly all churches get lumped together with the Church of England) is perceived as having been in a position of power and having used that power to press its beliefs on others, 'forcing' Christian morality on the nation.

Whether that is a fair understanding of the situation of past years, I doubt. However, that is beside the point. This is how it is perceived by many. Christianity has been part of 'the establishment'. And therefore Christians generally are looked upon as the oppressors – who resisted 'gay rights' and 'women's rights' and forced their faith on other cultures, just as valid as their own, through world mission. The fact that now Christians are the most persecuted and often most victimised group throughout the world, especially in Muslim and Communist countries, does not register. The facts of the on-going persecution of Christians in the twenty-first century have been shockingly under-reported in the secular press. The state church idea which seemed to put Christians in a good position for many hundreds of years has now backfired on us. Unsurprisingly, we find no hint of the idea of a state church in the New Testament.

So you see the corrosive results of political correctness. The reason for its destructiveness is that its very foundations bring it into conflict with reality. Having jettisoned the Biblical and common sense views of truth and justice, its only idea of justice is a flat total equality of outcome for everyone. But life is just not like that. Some people are more gifted than others – men and women are different, people make different choices in life, people do have different ideas and ambitions, some ideas of how to live are better than others. To make PC work you have to suppress the truth. The novelist Frederick Forsyth has said, 'I loathe and despise political correctness; basically because it is a lie.'

The Response to Political Correctness

How should Christians respond to political correctness? There might be a temptation to join in the game. For example, Christ encourages an unconditional compassion for the needy and many Christians have interpreted that in a PC way – identify the victims and support them and their interests, irrespective of other factors. Thus many Christians have dived into the *Make Poverty History* movement and called for the cancellation of Third World debt (and I have much sympathy with this movement), but with no comparable commitment to campaigning to get rid of corruption in African governments. But that is to break God's balance, his insistence on both compassion and truth, which we saw in the last chapter in the passage from Exodus.

Similarly, as things get tougher for Christians as this country becomes more and more PC, it might be thought that to protect ourselves we should try to play the 'more victimised than you' card. But the Bible tells us that our first priority must be truth, not manipulating situations to our own advantage. Yes, where Christians genuinely are victimised, let us speak up and bring the evidence. But we are not to try to claim 'victim status'. Truth must be our priority. Jesus said, 'If you hold to my teaching, you are really my disciples. Then you will know the truth, and the truth will set you free' (John 8:31-32).

Some Christian readers have to speak into situations in their work-places. Perhaps you are involved in a hospital or a school or local government in this PC world. Often there may be issues arising where political correctness comes into play in the discussions and decisions. Here are seven things to bear in mind as a Christian.

1. When you speak in public, make sure that what you say is factually correct. God is a God of truth and he honours the truth (Ps. 15:1-4).

2. Stick to rational, evidence-based arguments and encourage others to do the same. Where that does not happen, gently challenge the statements made.

3. Feel compassion for victims, but don't defer to them simply because they are needy. If their victim-hood is self-inflicted, deferring to them will not help in the long run.

4. Don't get into cultural relativism. The fact that someone is a victim or a minority does not excuse unethical behaviour you would not accept from other people. Remember Exodus 23:3 commands us, 'Do not show favouritism to a poor man in his lawsuit.'

5. Don't allow yourself to be made to feel guilty for something for which you are not responsible. For example, we in the West today are no more responsible for the slave trade of 200 years ago than present-day Germans are responsible for the holocaust, or present-day Muslims for the wars of Mohammed.

6. Listen carefully to the language used by PC spokesmen and spokeswomen. When they talk about 'equality', discern how they are using that word. What kind of equality have they fastened on to? Ask them exactly what they are talking about. Once we identify the way they are using the word, often their arguments are far easier to counter.

7. Remain faithful to God, just as Daniel did, living in the alien culture of Babylon.

Obviously, in a PC world this all takes courage. Pray for the Lord's strength.

The Gospel and Political Correctness

Lastly, thinking about PC leads us back to the gospel. Two words in many ways characterise PC. They are the words 'guilty' and 'victim'. It is no exaggeration to say that the perpetrators of political correctness set out to give victim status to their preferred groups and to make others feel guilty. It is interesting to reflect on those two concepts in the light of the good news of the Lord Jesus Christ.

First, think about guilt. Many people believe that PC has taken off, even though it is often so irrational, because people live on their feelings. Anthony Browne writes in *The Retreat of Reason*, 'In the battle between emotion and reason, emotion wins most of the time for most people…Few souls are tortured by bad reasoning; many are those tortured by guilt…Most people have a profound need to believe they are on the side of virtue.' Why is that? Why do we have this great desire to be 'in the right'? The Bible tells us that it is because we are not naked apes, the result of amoral evolution. In fact, we are inherently moral creatures made in the image of the holy God. And so it is that people 'show that the requirements of the law (of God) are written on their hearts, their consciences also bearing witness, and their thoughts now accusing, now even defending them' (Rom. 2:15).

But given this moral instinct written into our nature, we also find that we are all sinners. The condemnation of our consciences tells us we have done wrong. And that points to us being guilty before God. We have this deep desire to feel and know ourselves 'in the right' because there is a real need (more than psychological) to stand without guilt in the eyes of a holy God. We have a need to be justified. This means we need a Saviour. That Saviour is Jesus Christ, who died to make atonement for our sins and put us right with God.

Think *secondly* about the idea of 'the victim'. The logic of political correctness produces the 'powerful victim'. To be a victim gives you clout and power in a PC world. But of course the gospel reminds us of Christ – the victim. His death has made him powerful. This is not because everybody is made to feel sorry for him. Rather it is because through his unjust execution on the cross in our place, he has power to deal with our guilt before God and grant us forgiveness. Jesus is the truly 'powerful victim' who has power to deliver us from sin and its eternal consequences and set us free.

The apostle Paul tells us:

> [23]For all have sinned and fall short of the glory of God, [24]and are justified freely by his grace through the redemption that came by Christ Jesus. [25]God presented him as a sacrifice of atonement, through faith in his blood. He did this to demonstrate his justice, because in his forbearance he had left the sins committed beforehand unpunished— [26]he did it to demonstrate his justice at the present time, so as to be just and the one who justifies those who have faith in Jesus. (Rom. 3:23-26).

Chapter 5
Therapy culture:
the engine of political correctness

What is it that drives so many politically correct people to be quite aggressive towards those who disagree with them? Why has causing offence, even unintentionally, become such a big deal for them, almost in the category of criminal activity?

The answer is that in the new world of tacit atheism and post-modernism, personal emotions, feeling good about oneself and 'self-esteem' have become perhaps the most important things in the world.

In tracing the emergence of this kind of outlook it might be useful to begin by quoting a song from the 1960s by a songwriter who could almost be said to have shaped the thinking of his generation: Bob Dylan. These are the opening stanzas of his *Ballad of a Thin Man*:

> *You walk into the room*
> *With your pencil in your hand*
> *You see somebody naked*
> *You say, 'Who is that man?'*
> *You try so hard*
> *But you don't understand*
> *Just what you'll say when you get home*

Because something is happening here
But you don't know what it is
Do you, Mister Jones?

Dylan was very aware that times were changing, that a new outlook was surfacing during the sixties. The music was new, young people had money to spend, the pill had brought about a sexual revolution, drug culture was becoming more mainstream, ideas of morality and what life is about were altering. This song picks up perhaps some of the first inklings of the emergence of a post-modern outlook. Mr. Jones represents the old 'modern' outlook on life with its scientific approach and its search for objective truth; so he is described as entering the room with a pencil (and, we infer, perhaps a notebook). He is there to assess the 'happening' and analyse logically what is going on. But he is confronted by things which just do not make sense to him. Here is someone naked. Later in the song he is confronted by people answering his questions in irrational ways which just happen to rhyme with his own words. He is bewildered. These people are operating in ways which are out of the ordinary and which are completely alien to him. Hence, he doesn't comprehend. 'Something is happening here, but you don't know what it is, do you, Mr Jones?'

What is actually happening is that people are behaving to shock and get attention; reacting spontaneously and according to whatever makes them feel good in the immediate present. They live for the moment, for the transient 'high' they might experience through the risks they take and everyone's eyes being turned towards them. This is simply not the world of lawyers, and tax-deductible charities and professors, which Mr Jones is used to. It is more like some terrible freak-show circus. But actually, in the changed world he is entering, Mr Jones is the one who is seen as the freak.

Priority of experience

As we have already explained, when God is rejected, meaning in life tends to collapse. With no absolutes, no overarching story to make sense of the world, everything becomes a matter of personal opinion. This opens the way for post-modernism. Ultimately there are no rules. Mr Jones' world, in which you approach things rationally to lead you to the truth, is actually a figment of his imagination. And adopting the atheistic, post-modern view of life leaves you with only one thing worth living for, and that is to please yourself. What that comes down to in the last analysis is enjoying yourself and feeling good about yourself in whatever way you can. Hence we enter a new world where experiences, emotions and repairing damaged emotions take priority. We enter what has come to be known as a 'therapy culture'.

We can see immediately how this links into political correctness. If a person's life has no greater purpose than to feel good about themselves, then to cause offence, or even to raise questions in a way which might undermine their sense of self-esteem or make them feel bad about themselves, is the cardinal sin. We are seen as attacking what makes them tick as people. Just so, society has moved away from seeing good and evil in traditional moral terms. Good and evil are rewritten in emotional terms. To cause offence to someone, to damage their feelings, is to make them victims. This is true even if you did this unintentionally, just as much as if you unintentionally caused a serious car accident. Though you did not mean to do it, you would still be viewed as at fault.

Self-esteem

With the rise of this emotionally-centred world-view has come the rise of the therapy industry of counsellors, psychologists and psychiatrists.

Professor Frank Furedi of the University of Kent has described the upsurge of all this in his book *Therapy Culture*. For example, a search of 300 UK newspapers in 1980 did not find a single reference to the term 'self-esteem'. It found 3 citations in 1986. By 1990 this figure had risen to 103. A decade later, in 2000, there were a staggering 3,328 references. Similar figures apply for words like 'trauma', 'stress', and 'syndrome'.

In 1983 the psychiatrist M. Scott Peck, famous for his book *The Road Less Travelled,* published another book with the title *People of the Lie*. In many ways it was alerting us to the same shift from a moral culture to a therapy culture. His thesis was that neuroses develop where people seek to avoid legitimate responsibilities and the pain which goes with having failed in those responsibilities. The 'lie' which people try to live is that we are not moral beings. An evil person is consistently self-deceiving with the intent of avoiding guilt and maintaining an ability to think well of themselves – in our terms, to look after their self-esteem.

This witnesses to a tendency to reinterpret not just major difficulties but also normal experience through the medium of an emotional script, with the inevitable proliferation of psychological labels and therapeutic terms. We now take emotions very seriously. The old way of keeping your feelings under control is looked on with suspicion. The 'stiff upper lip' is frowned upon. Tears and emoting in public are what TV audiences now enjoy.

We have entered a world very different from what it was fifty or sixty years ago. This whole culture of emotion is bringing great changes to our society and also is affecting the churches.

Culture of Emotionalism

The emphasis that we put on 'feeling good about oneself' is a distinct feature of our contemporary Western world. You do not find this in, say, the rural parts of Africa. There, life is hard. People simply accept that some days are better than others; some days we feel good and some days we feel bad. That is how it is in a fallen world. But in the West, the necessity to 'feel good' flows from the atheistic outlook which has crept in that regards the individual self as the central focus of life. A sense of your own well-being is everything. There is nothing else to live for.

This priority given to positive emotions is very different from the traditional 'Protestant ethic' which the West adopted in the past and which saw hard work, sacrifice and discipline as virtues.

The acknowledgement of emotional pain through its public display is applauded today. This is looked upon as being 'authentic' as a person, showing who you really are. Hence the rise of 'confessional' TV shows like *Jerry Springer* etc, and the castigation of the Royal family when they desired not to make a public display of emotion over Princess Diana's death in 1997.

How did we get into this? The answer goes back, as we have said, to the rejection of the 'modern' world-view of science and reason and its being replaced by the post-modern outlook.

With no overall meaning or truth about the world, there is no faith or ideology worth living for, so living for self and positive feelings about oneself becomes the only possible purpose for life.

Just as in *Ballad of a Thin Man*, the therapeutic culture rejects both God and the ethos of rationality proclaimed by science (this is post-modernism). It makes life very individualistic, and the consumer society of shopping and accessories is there to help us all express our individuality. It only entertains faith in terms of a 'God' who is there to help the self. This is where churches are beginning to be affected. This is where the temptation arises to somehow reshape the gospel in order to make its main goal to make people feel better about themselves. But we will pick up on this in a later chapter.

Self-esteem: the cultural myth of our time

From this focus on emotion has grown up the whole counselling/therapy business, with its orientation towards making people feel better. The theory is that if people felt better about themselves, then they would behave better. In the popular way of thinking, low self-esteem is associated with virtually every ill that afflicts society – depression, domestic violence, misbehaviour at school, etc.

Once again, it is fairly clear how this attitude would support a politically correct approach to society. If you believe that it is low self-esteem which makes people behave badly, then the last thing you need to do is in any way criticise them. If you are concerned about threats posed by some Muslim groups, for example, then the one thing you must not do is to argue that their religion is wrong. This will only alienate and radicalise them further. Certainly, you must not evangelise them with the Christian gospel.

However, the idea that everyone will behave well if only we make them feel good about themselves is not only misguided but is leading to serious problems.

The Bible sees human beings as first of all moral beings before they are emotional beings. While there may be many contributing factors at a practical level, nevertheless the ultimate reason why people behave badly is that we are all fallen sinners. Since the first sin in the Garden of Eden, the whole human race has inherited the morally rebellious, self-centred nature of our father Adam. What people require in order to change is not an injection of self-esteem but a new birth by the power of the Holy Spirit through the Lord Jesus Christ. It is only as the sinful nature is met by the force of a new heart in Christ that people really begin to change for the better, and society with them. This is the message of the gospel: 'You must be born again' (John 3:7).

Given the power of the Holy Spirit in our lives, the gospel turns the assumption of therapy culture on its head. People will feel better when they believe and behave better (Prov. 1:8-9; Micah 6:8). The logic of cause and effect is reversed. We are to keep in step with the Spirit and so know his fruit in our lives. 'The fruit of the Spirit is love, joy, peace, patience, kindness, goodness, faithfulness, gentleness and self-control' (Gal. 5.22-23).

'The self-esteem deficit is a cultural myth that is continually promoted by its advocates,' says Frank Furedi, Professor of

Sociology at the University of Kent. Here are some of the reasons why.

- There is no agreed definition of self-esteem.

- People treat self-esteem as a 'magic bullet'. We should be suspicious of anything that is meant to be a 'magic bullet' which will solve all problems. It is unscientific. Human beings are very complex.

- In 1987 the California legislature set up a task force to investigate the links between low self-esteem and social problems. The result was that 'The association between self-esteem and its expected consequences are mixed, insignificant, or absent.'

- The growing disquiet about self-esteem took on real momentum with the school shootings at Columbine High School in the USA in April 1999. The killers, it seems, did not suffer from low self-esteem, as might be assumed, but from an unhealthy streak of individualism. In fact, some psychologists now argue that high self-esteem is linked to low self-control, which in turn can lead to violent behaviour.

Quoting Professor Furedi once again:'The truth is that feelings about oneself are mediated through complex relationships and institutions. Nor are these feelings static. They alter with changing events and opportunities. The attempt to treat self-esteem as an independent variable that determines broad patterns of behaviour requires a highly individualistic methodology that overlooks the broad context within which people interact with one another.'

The idea that building self-esteem should be the goal above all others at which we should aim simply does not fit the facts. But nevertheless it is the idea which drives many people and much of PC thinking. Yes, of course we want to nurture confident people. But the Bible is full of exhortations to find our confidence in God and his trustworthy love, not in ourselves. This is something very different from self-esteem. Massaging personal self-esteem will not solve our problems.

The last days

Sadly, not only society at large, but a slice of the Christian church has been deceived into buying in to the therapy culture standpoint. I want to say something about this as we close this chapter (though I will take it up again in chapter 10). The idea of making a priority of getting people to feel better about themselves seems so loving and so 'Christian'. The problem is not, as we shall see, that God is unconcerned about our emotions; but it is that therapy culture replaces God with the individual self. It is inherently man-centred and therefore idolatrous. Like all systems of idolatry, it is not only wrong, but cannot deliver on its promises.

The apostle Paul, writing to Timothy, seems to have prophetic insight into this in 2 Timothy 3:1-5:

> But mark this: There will be terrible times in the last days. [2] People will be lovers of themselves, lovers of money, boastful, proud, abusive, disobedient to their parents, ungrateful, unholy, [3] without love, unforgiving, slanderous, without self-control, brutal, not lovers of the good, [4] treacherous, rash, conceited, lovers of pleasure rather than lovers of God— [5] having a form of godliness but denying its power. Have nothing to do with them.

Here, Paul produces a list of sins that characterize the 'terrible times' of the 'last days' in which we live. There are two things to notice.

First, the list starts as if Paul is talking about society in general, 'People will be…' (verse 2). But he ends with a clear focus on the church: 'having a form of godliness but denying its power' (verse 5). The one merges into the other. The church has become worldly. You cannot see where the world ends and the church begins. It presents no contrast.

This becomes even clearer with the *second* point. Paul's list begins with two references to lovers (verse 2) and ends with two references to lovers (verse 4). And roughly in the middle there is another similar reference: 'not lovers of the good' (verse 3). Paul is making a devastating point. What makes a church fall into terrible times will be what it loves, or what it values. The misplaced loves of the church cause everything else which goes wrong.

Paul warns about three loves which go hand in hand with therapy culture.

Lovers of themselves (verse 2). In a church such as this, the spotlight will not be on loving God or on loving others, but on the individual and his or her needs. The object of worship in the church is actually the self. On Sunday people will arrive crushed, tired and bored, and it is seen as the church's task to ensure that they leave lifted, stimulated and feeling better. Such a church will be a great 'success'. But people arrive as lovers of self and leave as lovers of self.

Lovers of money (verse 2). There are crass versions of Christianity which claim that if Jesus were alive today he would wear designer tailoring and drive a Porsche, and that God wants us to be rich. I hope we know enough about the Bible and the sacrificial life of our Saviour to know that such a message is a horrible lie. But nevertheless we are tempted, and we live in a society which goes in for 'retail therapy' – buying things to make ourselves feel better.

Lovers of pleasure (verse 4). The key to the 'success' of this church is that it continually asks 'what do people like?' The first answer is that people like to be entertained. So the church packages everything in a way that is aimed to entertain. Second, this church makes sure that there is no demand which requires people to stop doing what they enjoy doing. This is because, in a therapy culture, the enjoyability of something is its highest justification. If it feels good, it is good. If it feels bad, it is bad. But this is to cut across some of the most essential elements of the gospel. Conviction of sin feels bad, but it is good, because it drives us to Christ in repentance. A church which follows this route will find it increasingly difficult to show how its members are different from the world, because at any point where its members have to choose between pleasure and Christ, the church capitulates.

But there is a fourth love, an all-important love, which is referred to by Paul.

Lovers of God (verse 4). Does all this mean that the church should be careless of how people feel and simply ignore hurts and pains? Not at all. But what it is saying is that 'feeling better' about ourselves must not become our purpose in life.

True Christianity certainly has a big emotional element. True Christian faith is about the heart and the affections. We are called to love God. We are called to joy and delight in him (Ps. 43:4; 73:25-26; Hab. 3:17-18). The trouble is that in allowing ourselves to become 'lovers of pleasure' we preclude ourselves from truly being 'lovers of God'.

The true purpose of our lives is to glorify God and enjoy him forever. In the goodness of God's character, the beauty of God's creation, and the grace of God's salvation, we are provided with every possible motive to desire and love him.

The object of our desires is not a psychological state called 'feeling good about myself'. We are to pursue joy in God, so that God gets all the glory. And as we do that by faith we will find that peace, joy and contentment which is indeed good for us (Phil.4:12-13). Jesus said, 'Seek first his kingdom and his righteousness, and all these things will be given to you as well' (Matt. 6:33).

Recommended reading:

Chris Green, *Finishing the Race: Reading 2 Timothy Today* (Sydney: Aquila Press, 2000)

Chapter 6
A guide to answering the gay agenda

Having given some thought to what political correctness is about, in the next four chapters we will investigate three areas of life in which PC has particular sway.

These are the areas of sexual orientation (particularly the gay lifestyle), the multi-faith society, and gender issues (with feminism particularly in mind). Our remit will be to try to give the salient points of what Scripture has to say in these areas and therefore how and why the Christian needs to stand firm against the pressures of PC. We begin with the issue of homosexuality.

The homosexual issue is an explosive one. To voice any reservations or disagreement with the direction of gay liberation almost inevitably invites attack and accusations of homophobia. In the summer of 2012, the deputy Prime Minister for the Coalition government and leader of the Liberal Democrat Party in the UK, Nick Clegg, made it quite clear that he thought that anyone who had any qualms of conscience over redefining marriage to include homosexual couples was 'a bigot'.

However, we must not be bamboozled by gay activists or our current permissive culture. We must seek to be Biblical, loving and rational in our stance. Enemies of historic Christian sex ethics can be found both inside and outside the church. Therefore we need to think about dealing with this issue both among professing Christians and in the secular world.

Arguing within the church

Within the church Scripture, as the word of God, must be our authoritative guide (2 Tim. 3:16-17). For those who claim to be within the church but do not accept Scripture, we need to move to the kind of arguments we will use later in the chapter for those outside the church. In his book *Issues Facing Christians Today*, John Stott identifies four groups of texts which mention the matter of homosexuality directly.

Genesis 19:1-13

[1] The two angels arrived at Sodom in the evening, and Lot was sitting in the gateway of the city. When he saw them, he got up to meet them and bowed down with his face to the ground. [2] "My lords," he said, "please turn aside to your servant's house. You can wash your feet and spend the night and then go on your way early in the morning." "No," they answered, "we will spend the night in the square." [3] But he insisted so strongly that they did go with him and entered his house. He prepared a meal for them, baking bread without yeast, and they ate. [4] Before they had gone to bed, all the men from every part of the city of Sodom—both young and old—surrounded the house. [5] They called to Lot, "Where are the men who came to you tonight? Bring them out to us so that we can have sex with them." [6] Lot went outside to meet them and shut the door behind him [7] and said, "No, my friends. Don't do this wicked thing. [8] Look, I have two daughters who have never slept with a man. Let

me bring them out to you, and you can do what you like with them. But don't do anything to these men, for they have come under the protection of my roof." [9] "Get out of our way," they replied. And they said, "This fellow came here as an alien, and now he wants to play the judge! We'll treat you worse than them." They kept bringing pressure on Lot and moved forward to break down the door. [10] But the men inside reached out and pulled Lot back into the house and shut the door. [11] Then they struck the men who were at the door of the house, young and old, with blindness so that they could not find the door. [12] The two men said to Lot, "Do you have anyone else here—sons-in-law, sons or daughters, or anyone else in the city who belongs to you? Get them out of here, [13] because we are going to destroy this place. The outcry to the LORD against its people is so great that he has sent us to destroy it."

Here we have an example of attempted homosexual gang rape (verse 5), which brings down the judgement of God. The original text uses the word *know*. The crowd wanted to 'know' those inside Lot's house. This word can have its natural meaning of simply 'becoming acquainted' with someone or something. But it is also used in Scripture of sexual relations (see for example Gen.4:1). Some gay sympathisers have expressed the idea that a desire for sexual relations was not involved here, but rather that the crowd were concerned to know whether the strangers who had been admitted to the town were hostile.

However, this construction is false. That Lot's daughters were (inexcusably) offered to the crowd implies a sexual connotation to the episode (verses 7-8). Further, the New

Testament book of Jude plainly interprets the actions of the men of Sodom in terms of sexual perversion (Jude 7).

But what is in view here is homosexual gang rape. It may be argued, understandably, that this text therefore does not pertain to 'loving' gay relationships. Therefore we must look further into Scripture.

> *Leviticus 18:22; 20:13*
> 'Do not lie with a man as one lies with a woman; that is detestable.'
>
> 'If a man lies with a man as one lies with a woman, both of them have done what is detestable. They must be put to death; their blood will be on their own heads.'

These texts, which clearly forbid men lying together as with a woman, are part of the holiness code for Israel. To get around them, the interpretation is put forward that the prohibition is not of ordinary homosexual acts, but of such acts performed in religious ritual.

However, the context is against such an approach. For example, a similar argument would then make 'ordinary' adultery (not performed in a religious setting) permissible (cf. Lev.18:20). This is plainly contrary to the seventh commandment (Exod. 20:14; Rom. 13:9). Therefore we cannot accept the 'religious ritual' argument concerning homosexual acts.

> *Romans 1:26-27*
> [26]Because of this, God gave them over to shameful lusts. Even their women exchanged natural relations for unnatural ones. [27]In the same way the men also

abandoned natural relations with women and were inflamed with lust for one another. Men committed indecent acts with other men, and received in themselves the due penalty for their perversion.

Here Paul speaks of homosexuality in terms of arising as a result of God's judgement on godless society, as he gives people up to go their own way (verses 24, 26, 28). The argument is brought that Paul is only referring to casual sex here and not to committed loving relationships. But that is to impose a distinction on the text which is not there. Paul just refers to homosexual acts, whether casual or not.

1 Corinthians 6:9-10; 1 Timothy 1:9-10
[9]Do you not know that the wicked will not inherit the kingdom of God? Do not be deceived: Neither the sexually immoral nor idolaters nor adulterers nor male prostitutes nor homosexual offenders [10]nor thieves nor the greedy nor drunkards nor slanderers nor swindlers will inherit the kingdom of God.

[9]We also know that law is made not for the righteous but for lawbreakers and rebels, the ungodly and sinful, the unholy and irreligious; for those who kill their fathers or mothers, for murderers, [10]for adulterers and perverts, for slave traders and liars and perjurers—and for whatever else is contrary to the sound doctrine

These are two lists of sins which are incompatible with the kingdom of God, the law of God and the gospel. Again, the argument is brought that these do not refer to committed loving relationships; but again there is no evidence for that. In the 1 Corinthians passage there are two Greek words relating to homosexuality.

Of these words Jim Packer has commented: '*arsenokoitai* means literally male bedders…the second, *malakoi* is used in many connections to mean unmanly, womanish and effeminate, and here refers to males matching the woman's part in physical sex' (Vestry Meeting at St. John's, Shaughnessy, Vancouver, 2002). Notice also here, praise the Lord, that Paul affirms that people can be saved and change from homosexual lifestyles as he tells the Corinthians, 'that is what some of you were' (1 Cor. 6:11).

Traditional Christian attitudes do not just hang on these few texts. The prohibitions of homosexual practice make sense only in the light of the positive teaching in Genesis 1 and 2 about human sexuality and heterosexual marriage – teaching specifically endorsed by our Lord Jesus Christ (Matt. 19:4-6).

This creation basis for sexual ethics answers the idea that the prohibitions of Scripture concerning homosexual acts were only relevant to the cultures of the Biblical times. Genesis is foundational for all human cultures. It speaks about the beginning of humanity and therefore applies to all humanity at all times. It also answers the idea that the 'love-quality' of a homosexual relationship is enough to justify it. True love is concerned with the highest welfare of the beloved, and how can it be loving to ignore our Maker's instructions for sexual relationships? (See Romans 13:9 etc.)

It is not because we do not care for or love those of homosexual orientation that we cannot accept that a sexually active gay lifestyle is okay. Neither is it because we hate adulterers that we believe that adultery is wrong. Neither is it because we have a phobia about lying that the church looks for truth. In all such cases and more, we are simply seeking to be faithful to what we believe the word of God to say. To resist the gay agenda is a matter of principle, not of personal malice. We believe that what the Scriptures teach should be the rule of faith and behaviour within the church.

Arguing outside the church

Christians interact with neighbours, colleagues, family and friends who are not Christians. Obviously just to quote the Bible to them will not suffice. They do not believe the Bible. How are we to rationally stand for God's ways in a way which will be helpful and make sense to them?

We believe God is loving. We believe that the laws which he has given are actually best in the long run for individuals and for human society. Therefore, once we know the facts, we should be in a position to put a case which is reasonable and will commend the Christian position. However, it may not deliver us from being called unkind, irrational and bigoted, since often (as we have pointed out in the chapter on post-modernism) if people cannot win arguments they simply try character assassination.

There are at least four areas where we can try to make reasonable points in this debate.

Genetics

Much headway has been made by the gay lobby by somehow bracketing their cause together with those concerning racial equality and women's liberation. Sometimes the impression has been given that sexual orientation is something like race or gender, written into a person's genetic make-up and an aspect of their lives over which they have no choice. Obviously if this were really the case the Biblical injunctions against homosexual activity would be grossly unfair.

However, this is not the case. Dr Peter May has written: 'Studies of identical twins have repeatedly shown that sexual orientation is not determined genetically. Identical twins with identical genes do not always have the same orientation. If one is homosexual, the other is far more likely to be heterosexual. Even though statistically, compared with the general population, there is an increased chance that the twin will be homosexual, this is far from guaranteed. So though there may be a genetic "tendency" toward homosexuality, sexual orientation is not genetically determined' (*Evangelicals Now*, September 2012).

This does not mean that same-sex attraction is reduced to a simple choice. Different people have different temptations. One man may find adultery with another man's wife a great temptation. Another might find other males attractive. But in neither case does that excuse us from taking responsibility for our behaviour. We are all accountable for the choices we make.

Health
Medical professionals are clear that homosexual activity is very dangerous. Professor Elizabeth Duncan writes: 'The shape of the bowel is not intended for the purpose of sexual intercourse. The muscle of the anal sphincter has to be forced open. The lining of the bowel is a single cell layer. As a result there is trauma and tearing. The semen action damages the bowel lining and the consequence is easy entrance to bacteria and viruses.' Even the Durex condom manufacturers, on their website, have advised against anal sex.

In a letter to the *Daily Telegraph* at the time of the Parliamentary debate over the lowering of the age of consent for homosexual acts, a group of doctors wrote: 'We believe that the health risks of anal sex, both heterosexual and homosexual, have been hushed up either because of a reluctance to speak about the subject, or by political correctness.' The letter went on to speak of the fact that homosexual activity is connected with premature death.

It is certainly true that compared, say, with the warnings given concerning the medical effects of smoking or drinking or obesity, comparatively little is said about the detrimental medical effects of sex outside of marriage generally, whether heterosexual or homosexual. But at the same time it is well known that there has been a huge increase in sexually transmitted diseases in Britain in recent years. It seems almost like a cover-up. Such is the power of political correctness with respect to sexual matters.

Family
Homosexual relationships are promoted as an 'alternative lifestyle'. This immediately asks a question of traditional family life. But historically it has always been some form of heterosexual marriage which has provided the backbone of every stable society. How can homosexual relationships be an 'alternative lifestyle' when there is no natural possibility of procreation? To put it bluntly, if all the world were gay, humanity would die out.

Further, the idea that to grow up in a homosexual family makes no difference to children (adopted or otherwise) is open to serious debate. In a recent project lesbian and single heterosexual mothers were recruited in the years 1976-77. The families were followed up in 1992-93, when their children were adults. Research found that fourteen of the twenty-five young adults reared in lesbian homes had considered having a lesbian or gay relationship, compared with only three of the twenty-one young adults reared by single heterosexual mothers. In addition, six of the twenty-five from lesbian homes had been involved in a sexual relationship with one or more people of the same sex, whereas none of those from heterosexual homes had had a same sex relationship (see Letters, *BMJ*, 24 August 2002).

Of course, some people may not be concerned if young people choose gay relationships. But the fact must be faced that there is a difference in the children. And if we take seriously the doctors' warnings of the health risks involved in homosexual acts, we ought to be concerned about young people getting into gay relationships.

Society
Many gay people are sensitive people and extremely caring towards others. But it can be argued that to choose a homosexual lifestyle precludes a person from contributing to the general good of society in various ways. For example, because of the health risks involved in homosexual sex, the UK Blood Transfusions Service will not accept blood from any man who has ever had sex with another man, even if it was 'safe sex' with a condom.

To disengage sex totally from procreation also brings difficulties to society. Over recent years the British government admitted for the first time that the decline in births may threaten National Insurance. In 2008 there were 3.8 people of working age for every person of pensionable age. This ratio is projected to fall to around 2.8 by the year 2033. We are finding it increasingly difficult to fund the support and care of elderly people. It would be inaccurate and wrong to say that the homosexual lifestyle alone is causing such difficulties. Much of youth culture promotes the same 'sex for fun, forget responsibility' outlook. But the gay philosophy is part of that individualistic and hedonistic outlook which is beginning to undermine society.

We will be castigated for doing so but, for the good of society generally, the Christian church needs to humbly stick to its Biblical position with respect to sexual ethics. We must lovingly try to support those who seek to follow Christ but struggle in the area of sexual identity and orientation, acknowledging that we are all sinners, far from perfect and constantly in need of the grace of God.

Chapter 7
Christianity and multiculturalism

On Monday 3 January 2000, leaders of nine religious faiths in Britain, including the then Archbishop of Canterbury, stood together in the Palace of Westminster in London for a 'Shared Act of Reflection and Commitment'.

Together they made a public statement which said: 'In a world scarred by the evils of war, racism, injustice and poverty', they would work together, 'to help bring about a better world now and for generations to come'. Tony Blair, the Prime Minister at that time, who hosted the gathering, described the occasion as 'progress of a very special sort'.

It is different faiths (both religious and non-religious) which give rise to different cultures. Different peoples' faith commitments give rise to the ideas which shape their way of life, their traditions, and the form of government their country has adopted. With increasing travel and migration of people to other countries there is a growing awareness that people of disparate backgrounds are now living in much closer proximity to one another than perhaps ever before, and we have got to learn to live together in peace. Perhaps it was with this in mind that Tony Blair looked upon the Palace of Westminster meeting as special progress. And now, in the aftermath of the 9/11 attacks in America and the 7/7 attacks in London by Islamist extremists, we can see the great importance of such progress.

There is a sense in which Christians rejoice in all the many races and in whatever is good in all the various cultures of the world. According to Scripture, all people are made in the image of God and are precious to him. We believe in the doctrine of common grace, which indicates that non-Christian cultures can often contain good things. Further, the book of Revelation gives us a vision of the end of time, with redeemed humanity from every nation, tribe and language gathered before the throne of God in worship and bringing the best of their people's 'splendour' (including culture?) into the city of God. This is the true family of man which makes the Christian heart race with excitement to the glory of Christ!

However, outside of Christ, our world, dominated by the ideology of political correctness, is adopting an approach to the problem of how different people can live together in peace which we label 'multiculturalism'. This way of dealing with the potential difficulties is proving both heavy-handed and actually a retrograde step. Thankfully, some people in government have been forced to have second thoughts about it. But we shall see what happens in future.

As Biblical Christians, we need to have some understanding of the multicultural programme and be aware of its dangers. We do want to live at peace with all people (Rom. 12:18). We do want to respect and serve others (Gal. 6:10). But we also believe it is right to have freedom of religion and free speech in a nation.

A history of pluralism

Before we get into the heart of this subject, we first need to note what is obvious. That is that a multicultural and religiously plural situation is nothing new for Christianity and for Biblical faith. In the Old Testament times the people of the LORD were surrounded by nations who worshipped other gods. Egypt, Babylon, Philistia and many more had their own religions. Generally speaking, each nation or ethnic group had its own god, and the culture of their land was based on this. To begin with, Old Testament nations tended to be fairly isolationist and monochrome in their culture. But by the time we get to Nebuchadnezzar and the Babylonian conquests and deportations, there seems to have been something of an experiment in multiculturalism (Dan. 3.7; Esth. 1.8).

However, when we move into the age of the New Testament, the multicultural idea had very much taken off. We find that cities and countries contained a variety of people, religions and cultures. Under the aegis of the Roman empire there had been much migration between the different lands surrounding the Mediterranean. Migrants had brought their own religions to different places and each region or city hosted a number of contrasting cults and faiths. So long as you acknowledged Caesar as Lord, you were left alone.

The Jews had scattered across many lands; and in most cities there was a Jewish synagogue alongside temples of Greek gods and goddesses and others. We can think of the apostle Paul visiting Athens and finding it religiously hugely diverse, with shrines and altars of many kinds everywhere (Acts 17:22-23).

It was against such a multi-faith and multicultural background that the early church 'turned the world upside down' for

Christ. So living with pluralism, amidst a plurality of faiths and cultures, is in itself nothing new for Christians. Our God is able to sustain his church and even cause it to grow marvellously within such an environment.

Descriptive and prescriptive

The situation I have sketched out in the Acts of the Apostles is usually referred to as 'descriptive pluralism'. It was simply the situation. It was simply what pertained in those days.

But what is new is what has come to be termed 'prescriptive pluralism'. This is the idea that a multiplicity of faiths and cultures is not just an observable fact in various countries, but is something which is theoretically justified and that all religions ought to be promoted as equally valid. This is the approach adopted by multiculturalism.

On the surface this sounds right and good. But the corollary of this is taken to be that therefore anyone or any group which claims to have 'the truth' in such a way that other faiths are deemed untrue or wrong is not to be tolerated. Such a group might offend others. For PC this is looked upon as abominable and labelled as some kind of religious fascism.

It is this 'prescriptive pluralism' which is at the heart of the multicultural programme. This outlook would want to legislate restrictions on what people, especially Bible-believing Christians, are allowed to believe and are allowed to declare publicly. This prescriptive pluralism therefore becomes an attack on free speech and liberty. Inevitably, it comes into collision with those who believe in Jesus, who said, 'I am the way and the truth and the life. No one comes to the Father except through me' (John 14.6).

Taking offence

The politically correct go to town at this point. They believe that they know what will offend people of various faiths and therefore seek to bring restrictions on how one faith may or may not express its religion at various festivals. Christians have particularly suffered from this kind of imperious being dictated to. Some companies have deemed it offensive for a Christian even to wear a small cross with their uniforms. 'You must not do that. It will offend the Hindus.' 'You must not wear that symbol. It will upset the Muslims.' As we have noted earlier, often when the Hindus or the Muslims are asked about what we have been told will offend them, they have answered that it would do nothing of the sort.

But politically correct people are using the idea of potential offence to shut down debate and to challenge freedom of speech. This is what appears to have happened recently on university campuses in Britain. Christian Unions have historically often been the biggest voluntary societies on campus. They have stood for evangelical faith; and though their meetings are open to all, they have required those who join as members – or at least those who take positions of leadership in the CU – to show their agreement with a simple doctrinal statement. However, politically correct university administrators and student unions see this as offensive and non-inclusive. Legal moves have been made to stop the Christian Unions maintaining their doctrinal commitments.

Now, of course no one should set out deliberately to offend other people. But there are two things to say. *First,* there is a definite difference between expressing differing points of view and abusing people who think differently from ourselves. To disagree with someone is not to insult them. When a group of people are not allowed to define their membership by a set of beliefs, political correctness has become oppression. *Secondly,* we need to cultivate a tolerant society in which people do not easily take offence. Sadly, it seems to be true that in this politically correct environment some minority groups have been willing to make the most of a supposed 'offence' in order to raise their profile or strengthen their position over against others.

How multiculturalism brings trouble

Racial equality is taken as a given in the Biblical world-view. All people of whatever race are traced back to the first human couple God created, Adam and Eve (Acts 17:26). Therefore, all individuals of whatever race or language are equally valuable in God's sight.

But multiculturalism is not about the racial equality of human beings. Multiculturalism seeks to insist that all *cultures* are equally valid. It is trying to say that all *faiths* must recognize each other as equally true. This needs to be borne in mind. We must not confuse the two. Race is one thing. Culture or faith is another.

Multiculturalism is no doubt well intentioned. It has the goal of different peoples living in peace together. However, in practice it tends to bring trouble. It does not bring about respect between different groups, but tends to promote rivalry.

How does multiculturalism produce difficulty? Let me cite a well-known example. The experience of the community in Bradford, West Yorkshire, as told by the veteran anti-fascist campaigner Kenan Malik provides a salutary example.

In April 1976, twenty-four people were arrested following a riot between Asian youths and National Front demonstrators. As a result of this racist conflict, the Asian Youth Movement was formed in an attempt to protect Asians from white racists. They argued that they were acting in self-defence and won their court cases.

Consequently, Bradford Council, aware of the Asian community's growing militancy, drew up equal-opportunity statements, established race relations units, and began a programme of funding Asian organisations. The Council declared that every section of its community had 'an equal right to maintain its own identity, culture, language, religion and customs'.

Following this in 1981, in an attempt to placate militant religious leaders, the Council then aided and helped fund the Bradford Council of Mosques. But, worried that they might appear to be showing bias in doing this, the Council then felt it should set up the Federation of Sikh Organisations and the Vishwa Hindu Parishad, which it did in 1984. Kenan Malik says, 'The consequence was to create division and tensions within and between different Asian communities, as each fought for a greater allocation of Council funding.' Since World War II people of different races had lived peacefully alongside each other across the city of Bradford. But by the mid-1980s the Asian community had begun to fragment along religious lines. Muslims began to live in one area, Sikhs in another,

109

Hindus in another. They began having separate schools and working for separate businesses. The Council's well-meaning, politically correct, multicultural approach had actually led to less harmony in the city rather than more. Commenting on the Bradford story, journalist Patrick West has said that the multicultural approach resulted in different religious groups 'living isolated, parallel lives in a climate of mutual suspicion and antagonism'.

With its programme of taking positive steps to maintain the 'equality' of cultures, what multiculturalism actually does is to produce a politically correct apartheid. Interestingly, this seems not to match the desires of the British people. A September 2004 poll for YouGov showed that both white and non-white Britons did actually prefer integration, with 70% of whites believing ethnic minorities were too isolated, and 65% of respondents from ethnic minorities agreeing.

The hypocrisy of prescriptive pluralism

There is a vast amount which could be said about what is wrong with prescriptive pluralism, but let me simply indicate three fatal flaws in its logic.

It is a biased agenda

Multiculturalism often promotes itself under the banner of being ethnically and religiously sensitive. If you, perhaps as a Christian, give your view of a subject, you will be smiled at paternalistically by the politically correct person and told, 'Well, that is just your perspective.' The implication is, 'You are biased, but I am not.' But actually the whole exercise is biased. It is biased towards Western secularism, which is the mother of political correctness. 'All cultures are equal,' we are told.

But the question is, 'Who says so?' Does a Muslim believe that? Does a Hindu not believe that her way is right? Does a Christian not believe that Christian behaviour is the best path to follow? In fact, it is only the Western secularist who believes that all cultures are equal. So the agenda is biased from the start.

Or come at it through the religious route. 'All religions are of equal value,' we are told. But how do you define 'religion'? You cannot just say, for example, that religions are about belief in God or gods. Many Buddhists do not believe in divine persons. I remember the story of a Christian missionary giving a Bible to an Indian Hindu intellectual. After he had read it, the man said, 'I thought you said this was a religious book? As far as I can see it is not about religion. It is a particular interpretation of history.' So in his own terms of ritual, etc., this man did not recognize Christianity as a religion. Now, how does the multi-faith agenda define religion? Basically, it defines it as anything that is not Western secularism. It will not include itself. This is pure bias.

It is an irrational agenda
The multicultural agenda wishes us to believe that all faiths and cultures are equally valid. It does this out of a concern for human rights.

But at the same time there are certain faiths and cultures which do not match or which actually attack the human rights which the politically correct say they are seeking to uphold. Let me take two extreme examples simply to prove the point.

During the 1930s the philosophy of Nazism took root in Germany, with Adolf Hitler being swept into power. But

111

Nazism, based on a version of social Darwinism, believed that the Arian race was the 'master race' and that other races (like the Jews) were inferior. Nazism therefore promoted a culture of racism which led to the tragedy of the holocaust. Here then is a culture which opposes multiculturalism. For the politically correct to say that all people and cultures are equal is irrational and ludicrous if they include cultures (like Nazism) which say they are not.

But it is not just Nazism which has such a view. The late radical Islamist Osama bin Laden took an equivalent position. Interviewed on the Arabic news station *Al-Jazeera* after the attacks of 9/11 on the Pentagon and the World Trade Centre in New York, he made clear his hatred of Western culture. Commenting on what he hoped the attacks really meant, he let out an elated cry, saying, 'The values of this Western civilization under the leadership of America have been destroyed. Those awesome symbolic towers which speak of liberty, human rights and humanity have been destroyed. They have gone up in smoke.' Notice what he abhors: liberty and human rights. He would see those, presumably, as a challenge to the absolute authority of Allah and therefore to be repudiated.

Here then again is an attitude and (with extremist Islam) a culture which deplores another culture. How can such a culture sit rationally within an outlook which says 'all cultures are equal'? It cannot.

Most multiculturalists, I think, would rightly reject both Nazism and bin Laden's form of extreme Islam. But if that is the case, it is plain that they are bringing certain criteria to bear in considering what is an acceptable culture and what is not. In other words, they are contradicting the idea that all cultures are equal.

It is an imperialistic agenda

In considering different faiths there is a famous parable or story to which people often refer. It is the story of a number of blind men touching and feeling different parts of an elephant and trying to describe the animal. One reports his feeling of naked solid bone – the tusk. Another speaks of a sturdy flexible cylinder – the trunk. Another indicates a smaller, thinner appendage – the tail. Another speaks of a large high wall – the body. On the basis of their contrasting experiences, they argue with each other and contradict each other as to what the animal is like. But the king, looking on, tells them that they are wrong to argue. They are all touching the same animal, but just different parts of it. 'There,' says the multi-faith/multicultural outlook, 'you religious people are all blind. Even though you have such contrasting ideas, you are all in touch with the same reality and therefore should acknowledge that each person's point of view is equally valid.' It all appears so reasonable.

But listen to what Bishop Lesslie Newbiggin says in *The Gospel in a Pluralist Society*:

> In the famous story of the blind men and the elephant…
> the real point of the story is constantly overlooked. The
> story is told from the point of view of the king and his
> courtiers, who are not blind but can see that the blind
> men are unable to grasp the full reality of the elephant
> and are only able to get hold of part of it. The story
> is constantly told to neutralise the affirmations of the
> great religions, to suggest that they learn humility and
> recognize that none of them can have more than one
> aspect of the truth. But, of course, the real point of the
> story is the exact opposite. If the king were also blind,

there would be no story. The story is told by the king, and it is the immensely arrogant claim of one who sees the full truth, which all the world's religions are only groping after. It embodies the claim to know the full reality which relativizes all the claims of the religions.

The multicultural programme assumes the position of the king. It is therefore very much a kind of imperialistic agenda. 'We know what is right and you religious people must do as we say.' In particular, it is the arrogant claim of the politically correct that religious people must give up believing or declaring that they have found universal truth.

Once we step back and look at all this, we see just how hypocritical the politically correct multicultural programme actually is. This is because it is itself actually guilty of all the things of which it accuses the religions (and especially Christianity). It is biased; it is biased towards Western secularism. It is irrational; it says that all cultures must be treated as equal, when it clearly would reject cultures which reject common human rights. It is imperialistic; it decries those who proclaim they have universal truth, but at the same time it says that all must bow to its agenda.

A Biblical appraisal

What is the Biblical approach to other faiths and cultures? Scripture makes it clear that faith in Jesus Christ is the only way of salvation for all the world (John 14:6; Acts 4:12). Hence the church's great commission is to take the gospel message to all nations with a view to their conversion to Christ. But having insisted on this stance, there are four Biblical considerations which must inform and govern our attitude to people of other cultures and faiths. We can disagree with people while still very much loving and respecting them as human beings.

The creation of God
The God of the Bible is revealed to us as the Creator. More than this, because the world is the work of his hands, all the universe speaks of him, his existence and his glory (Ps. 19:1-4; Rom. 1:20). When Paul spoke to the pagan philosophers on Mars Hill in ancient Athens, he specifically referred to this revelation of God in creation and told his listeners that 'God did this so that men would seek him and perhaps even reach out for him and find him, though he is not far from each one of us' (Acts 17:27). This means that Christians should not despise other faiths and cultures. People are lost, and through the evidence of God in creation may be doing their best, in their terms, to reach out for God. What creation tells them about God cannot save them. We cannot read the gospel in the stars. We cannot learn of Christ in the marvellous mountain panoramas of the earth. But nevertheless these things do speak of the Creator; and in some way other religions can be a sincere response to that. This is not to be despised, but rather to be respected.

The love of God
The apostle Paul encourages churches to pray for the good of all people, and then says: 'This is good, and pleases God our Saviour, who wants all men to be saved and to come to a knowledge of the truth. For there is one God and one mediator between God and men, the man Christ Jesus, who gave himself as a ransom for all men – the testimony given in its proper time' (1 Tim. 2:3-6). Though Scripture teaches that not all will be saved, nevertheless God in his love wishes that all would be saved. In this sense, all people are the objects

115

of God's love. His displeasure with us all because of our sin does not negate this love. Rather, the fact that he still loves despite our sin shows the intensity of his love. However, the point which is germane to our discussion is simply that if God has a love for all people of whatever race or creed, then the Christian too is called to love and treat others with respect. We do not agree with them, but we can respect and appreciate them.

The law of God

But having said this, the Bible does not have a blanket approach to all other faiths and cultures. The living God is holy. The holiness of his character is expressed through his moral law. This means that some religions or sects may be particularly obnoxious to God since they involve some gross violation of his commands. Thus the cults of Old Testament Canaan with their practice of child sacrifice were especially abhorrent to God, and after giving these people much time to turn away from these practices, God eventually called his people Israel to destroy them. Just as most people would see that World War II had to be fought to stop the Jewish holocaust, so these wars had to be fought to stop such atrocious practices.

However, elsewhere in Scripture we find other approaches to other faiths which do not violate God's moral sensibilities in such flagrant ways. All are judged by God's law.

We might think of the beliefs of the wise men (or Magi) who were led to Bethlehem to find the baby Jesus by a mysterious star. Though their philosophy-cum-faith, as it stood, was insufficient to save them – that is why they were led to the Christ-child – nevertheless God did deal with them through it. Or again, think of the devout Roman centurion, Cornelius, whom we meet in the New Testament book of Acts. He was drawn to the Jewish faith, supporting the synagogue. Yet he was not saved and so still needed Christ. But God sent an angel to this sincere man of prayer to tell him to invite Peter to come and preach the good news about Jesus to him and his whole household. So it was that Cornelius found Christ. As it was, his religion was insufficient. He was not saved. Nevertheless, God took note of him and so graciously led him to salvation. Before becoming a Christian Cornelius had no saving religion, but nevertheless we must see that God warmed to his seeking heart; and obviously his religion was in a totally different category in God's eyes from that of the Old Testament Canaanites.

So it is that Christians are called to be discerning about different faiths. There is much good in some. There is much which may be totally unacceptable in others. We are to make such assessments not in terms of our own personal likes and dislikes, but in terms of God's moral law.

The grace of God
According to the Bible, the Christian has only become a Christian by the pure grace of God. We have not become Christians because we were wiser than others, or because we were better than others. Left to ourselves, we would never have opened our hearts to Christ.

We were as blind and deaf towards God as anyone else in the world. Therefore it is totally inappropriate for the Christian to look down on those who have not yet seen the truth and accepted the Lord Jesus Christ. Without the intervention of God in our lives by his Holy Spirit, we would still be in the same condition as them.

These four considerations make it imperative for Christians to treat others who may differ from us with grace and with respect. There will be times when we have to disagree with people. We may have to do so vehemently at times. But though we may disagree with what they stand for, we are called to love them as people.

Living in peace?

The Bible speaks with common sense when it asks 'Do two walk together unless they have agreed to do so?' (Amos 3:3). In order for people of varying outlooks to live together peacefully there needs to be an agreement between the different parties. There needs to be a consensus concerning the government of the public behaviour of all communities which is recognized as just and (as far as possible) for the good of every individual and for society as a whole.

This consensus requires two things. It requires a combination of law and tolerance. If there is no law about how people from different sections of society treat each other then, given the track record of human nature, this will most certainly lead to abuse. On the other hand, to try to legislate for every little offence which might occur as one community's behaviour or attitude might ruffle the feathers of another person would be to invite increasing litigation between communities and would only inflame strained relationships. Minor offences need to be shrugged off and tolerated. Only with such a balance of law and goodwill can society be both free and safe for different communities.

The obvious question concerns where the line is to be drawn. Where must law end and tolerance be encouraged to come into play? This is obviously a vast subject. But from a Biblical point of view, the problem is not too difficult. Different communities need to discuss together and agree together on a way forward together as a society. This may seem problematic, but I think it can be assumed that all people of goodwill would want to see laws which forbid violence or the incitement of violence against others, and which uphold justice in terms of the bodily well-being of everyone. But at the same time, all people of goodwill would want, within those parameters, to uphold freedom of conscience and freedom of speech. We want a society in which there is respect and free discussion of ideas.

In other words, violence should be rejected by all and there ought to be laws which insist that people of different backgrounds cannot be discriminated against with respect to where they can live or how they can earn their living or receive health care, simply because they come from a different community. This is common justice. It is common justice which secures a peaceful society.

The problem with PC

However, to try to bring legislation which goes further than this is to bring trouble. Legislation which tries to regulate people's thought patterns, or to protect people from any kind of emotional upset, or which insists that a person's conscience or their peaceful public expression of their beliefs must be over-ridden in favour of the desires of those of a different community is to go too far. It is to try to impose law where law is out of its depth. This is the problem with political correctness. It thinks that all problems can be solved by law. But that is not true. To bring law into areas of life where it is inappropriate will only lead to a build-up of resentment.

Chapter 8
Pluralism, inclusivism and the gospel

The tacit atheism of our age has led to the idea that there is no revelation from heaven, no word from Almighty God, and all religions are therefore just matters of opinion, equally valid. This, of course, is the viewpoint of the secular Westerner, not of those within the various faiths.

Faiths and sects abound today. In Athens Paul found all kinds of 'gods' worshipped in the city. In that sense, as we noted in the previous chapter, from early times the world has been 'pluralist', with many faiths rather just one. But now, under the pressures of secularism and political correctness, we see a change from this 'descriptive pluralism' to 'prescriptive pluralism'. Every faith must accept every other faith as valid. No single religion has the right to call itself the truth and claim to be the only way of salvation. This is an affront to other people's beliefs. Some believe that the public questioning of certain faiths should be criminalised and Christian evangelism classified as a hate crime. In January 2006 the 'Religious Hatred Bill' almost passed through the House of Commons, but was defeated, quite miraculously, by just one vote.

This 'prescriptive pluralism' is a great threat to Bible churches, which proclaim concerning the Lord Jesus, 'Salvation is found in no one else, for there is no other name under heaven given to men by which we must be saved' (Acts 4:12). Feeling the potential clash that such a 'narrow' view of the gospel might bring with our pluralist world, people inside the church have dreamed up a number of approaches to try to circumvent the problem, so that Biblical Christianity might be interpreted in a more all-embracing way.

Two questions and three positions

Two questions have to be faced. First, *Is Jesus Christ the only Saviour?* More fully: Is the sinless life of the God-man Jesus Christ and his atoning death and resurrection the sole means by which the penalty of human sin is paid and we are reconciled to God? Second, *Is personal faith in Christ necessary to be saved?* Is conscious knowledge of Christ's death and resurrection and explicit faith in him as our Saviour needed for anyone to be reconciled to God? There has been much waffling on these questions, even from people who call themselves evangelicals.

It is possible to give three different answers to this combination of questions. The pluralist would answer 'No' to both questions. The inclusivist would answer 'Yes' to the first question and 'No' to the second. The Biblical Christian (Exclusivist) answers 'Yes' to both questions.

Christ alone?

Scripture makes it quite clear that Jesus is the only way of salvation (John 14:6; Acts 4:10-12; 1 Tim. 2:5). It proclaims this on the basis of five great truths about Jesus. These truths show him to be unique, and therefore the only possible Saviour for mankind.

1) His virgin conception

Therefore the Lord himself will give you a sign: The virgin will be with child and will give birth to a son, and will call him Immanuel. (Isa. 7:14)

[18]This is how the birth of Jesus Christ came about: His mother Mary was pledged to be married to Joseph, but before they came together, she was found to be with child through the Holy Spirit. [19]Because Joseph her husband was a righteous man and did not want to expose her to public disgrace, he had in mind to divorce her quietly. [20]But after he had considered this, an angel of the Lord appeared to him in a dream and said, 'Joseph son of David, do not be afraid to take Mary home as your wife, because what is conceived in her is from the Holy Spirit. [21]She will give birth to a son, and you are to give him the name Jesus, because he will save his people from their sins.' [22]All this took place to fulfil what the Lord had said through the prophet: [23]'The virgin will be with child and will give birth to a son, and they will call him Immanuel'—which means, 'God with us.' [24]When Joseph woke up, he did what the angel of the Lord had commanded him and took Mary home as his wife. [25]But he had no union with her until she gave birth to a son. And he gave him the name Jesus. (Matt. 1:18-25)

[26]In the sixth month, God sent the angel Gabriel to Nazareth, a town in Galilee, [27]to a virgin pledged to be married to a man named Joseph, a descendant of David. The virgin's name was Mary. [28]The angel went to her and said, 'Greetings, you who are highly favoured! The Lord is with you.' [29]Mary was greatly troubled at his words and wondered what kind of greeting this might

be. [30]But the angel said to her, 'Do not be afraid, Mary, you have found favour with God. [31]You will be with child and give birth to a son, and you are to give him the name Jesus. [32]He will be great and will be called the Son of the Most High. The Lord God will give him the throne of his father David, [33]and he will reign over the house of Jacob forever; his kingdom will never end.' [34]'How will this be,' Mary asked the angel, 'since I am a virgin?' [35]The angel answered, 'The Holy Spirit will come upon you, and the power of the Most High will overshadow you. So the holy one to be born will be called the Son of God. [36]Even Elizabeth your relative is going to have a child in her old age, and she who was said to be barren is in her sixth month. [37]For nothing is impossible with God.' [38]'I am the Lord's servant,' Mary answered. 'May it be to me as you have said.' Then the angel left her. (Luke 1:26-38)

The virgin conception lays the foundation for Jesus' incarnation as the God-man. The Holy Spirit replaced the human father in conception so that in his humanity Jesus is both son of Mary and Son of God. Also the virgin conception secures his sinlessness. Sin has infected the whole human race through Adam, who is the head of fallen humanity (Rom. 5:12, 18). But for Jesus, though truly human (seed of the woman, Gen. 3:15), Adam is not his head; and therefore he is without sin and so able to carry our sin. This is true of Jesus only.

2) His historical incarnation
[1]In the beginning was the Word, and the Word was with God, and the Word was God. [2]He was with God in the beginning. [3]Through him all things were made; without him nothing was made that has been made. [4]In him was

life, and that life was the light of men. [5]The light shines in the darkness, but the darkness has not understood it.

[6]There came a man who was sent from God; his name was John. [7]He came as a witness to testify concerning that light, so that through him all men might believe. [8]He himself was not the light; he came only as a witness to the light. [9]The true light that gives light to every man was coming into the world. [10]He was in the world, and though the world was made through him, the world did not recognize him. [11]He came to that which was his own, but his own did not receive him. [12]Yet to all who received him, to those who believed in his name, he gave the right to become children of God— [13]children born not of natural descent, nor of human decision or a husband's will, but born of God. [14]The Word became flesh and made his dwelling among us. We have seen his glory, the glory of the One and Only, who came from the Father, full of grace and truth. [15]John testifies concerning him. He cries out, saying, 'This was he of whom I said, "He who comes after me has surpassed me because he was before me."' [16]From the fullness of his grace we have all received one blessing after another. [17]For the law was given through Moses; grace and truth came through Jesus Christ. [18]No one has ever seen God, but God the One and Only, who is at the Father's side, has made him known. (John 1:1–18)

[1]In the past God spoke to our forefathers through the prophets at many times and in various ways, [2]but in these last days he has spoken to us by his Son, whom he appointed heir of all things, and through whom he made the universe. [3]The Son is the radiance of God's glory and the exact representation of his being, sustaining

all things by his powerful word. After he had provided purification for sins, he sat down at the right hand of the Majesty in heaven. (Heb. 1:1-3)

[5]Your attitude should be the same as that of Christ Jesus: [6]Who, being in very nature God, did not consider equality with God something to be grasped, [7]but made himself nothing, taking the very nature of a servant, being made in human likeness. [8]And being found in appearance as a man, he humbled himself and became obedient to death—even death on a cross! [9]Therefore God exalted him to the highest place and gave him the name that is above every name, [10]that at the name of Jesus every knee should bow, in heaven and on earth and under the earth, [11]and every tongue confess that Jesus Christ is Lord, to the glory of God the Father. (Phil. 2:5-11)

Only one who is both God and man can be our Saviour. He had to be God in order to accomplish our salvation. The penalty for sin against the infinite God is infinite. Only an infinite person could deal with it in a conclusive and final way. He had to be man, since only as man could he represent human beings and stand in our place before God (that is why the Old Testament sacrifices could not achieve salvation). The question then is, 'Who else is both God and man?' The answer is 'No one'.

3) His sinless life
God made him who had no sin to be sin for us, so that in him we might become the righteousness of God. (2 Cor. 5:21)

For we do not have a high priest who is unable to sympathise with our weaknesses, but we have one who has been tempted in every way, just as we are – yet was without sin. (Heb. 4:15)

[21]To this you were called, because Christ suffered for you, leaving you an example, that you should follow in his steps. [22]'He committed no sin, and no deceit was found in his mouth.' [23]When they hurled their insults at him, he did not retaliate; when he suffered, he made no threats. Instead, he entrusted himself to him who judges justly. [24]He himself bore our sins in his body on the tree, so that we might die to sins and live for righteousness; by his wounds you have been healed. (1 Peter 2:21-24)

Jesus had to live a sinless life so that he could present himself as a sinless sacrifice on our behalf. But also he had to live a sinless life in order to succeed on our behalf where Adam failed. The temptation of Christ in the desert parallels the temptation of Adam and Eve in the Garden of Eden. But where they failed, he was victorious over Satan. His active obedience is counted ours. The negative of our sin is taken away by the cross. But that would only, as it were, bring us back to 'zero' in God's sight. However, the perfect life of Jesus is counted as ours so that we are positively justified and reckoned righteous in God's sight. History shows us no one else who has lived a sinless life and therefore is equipped to be our Saviour.

4) His substitutionary death
[4]Surely he took up our infirmities and carried our sorrows, yet we considered him stricken by God, smitten by him, and afflicted. [5]But he was pierced for our transgressions, he was crushed for our iniquities; the punishment that

brought us peace was upon him, and by his wounds we are healed. [6]We all, like sheep, have gone astray, each of us has turned to his own way; and the LORD has laid on him the iniquity of us all. (Is. 53:4-6)

[23]for all have sinned and fall short of the glory of God, [24]and are justified freely by his grace through the redemption that came by Christ Jesus. [25]God presented him as a sacrifice of atonement, through faith in his blood. He did this to demonstrate his justice, because in his forbearance he had left the sins committed beforehand unpunished— [26]he did it to demonstrate his justice at the present time, so as to be just and the one who justifies those who have faith in Jesus. (Rom. 3:23-26)

[10]All who rely on observing the law are under a curse, for it is written: 'Cursed is everyone who does not continue to do everything written in the Book of the Law.' [11]Clearly no one is justified before God by the law, because, 'The righteous will live by faith.' [12]The law is not based on faith; on the contrary, 'The man who does these things will live by them.' [13]Christ redeemed us from the curse of the law by becoming a curse for us, for it is written: 'Cursed is everyone who is hung on a tree.' [14]He redeemed us in order that the blessing given to Abraham might come to the Gentiles through Christ Jesus, so that by faith we might receive the promise of the Spirit. (Gal. 3:10-14)

Isaiah foretold that Christ would be 'pierced for our transgressions'. The events of the Passion make it clear that Jesus died in the place of Barabbas (Mark 15:6-15), again picturing substitution. Paul tells us that Christ 'died for our sins' (1 Cor. 15:3) and that 'God made him who had no sin to be sin for us' (2 Cor. 5:21). If this is not true, there is no good news – we have to fall back into the crippling impossibility of 'salvation by works'. But the question is, 'Is there any other death like that of Jesus which atones for our sins?' The answer is 'No'. Jesus alone has done this.

5) His triumphant resurrection

[22]Men of Israel, listen to this: Jesus of Nazareth was a man accredited by God to you by miracles, wonders and signs, which God did among you through him, as you yourselves know. [23]This man was handed over to you by God's set purpose and foreknowledge; and you, with the help of wicked men, put him to death by nailing him to the cross. [24]But God raised him from the dead, freeing him from the agony of death, because it was impossible for death to keep its hold on him. (Acts 2:22-24)

He was delivered over to death for our sins and was raised to life for our justification. (Rom. 4:25)

[1]Now, brothers, I want to remind you of the gospel I preached to you, which you received and on which you have taken your stand. [2]By this gospel you are saved, if you hold firmly to the word I preached to you. Otherwise, you have believed in vain. [3]For what I received I passed on to you as of first importance: that Christ died for our sins according to the Scriptures, [4]that he was buried, that he was raised on the third day according to the Scriptures, [5]and that he appeared to Peter, and then to the Twelve. [6]After that, he appeared

to more than five hundred of the brothers at the same time, most of whom are still living, though some have fallen asleep. [7]Then he appeared to James, then to all the apostles, [8]and last of all he appeared to me also, as to one abnormally born. (1 Cor. 15:1-8)

Look at 1 Corinthians 15:3-5, the last passage quoted above. The resurrection of Christ is not presented as a religious myth. It is presented as a fact. Jesus died; and the empirical evidence for that is that he was buried. He rose again; and the empirical evidence is that he was seen. And 1 Corinthians 15:17 says 'And if Christ has not been raised, your faith is futile; you are still in your sins.' Here is the connection between the efficacy of Christ's death and the resurrection. His death is the payment; his resurrection is the receipt. His resurrection demonstrates that our sins have been fully paid for. Who else is risen from death? Once again, we see that Jesus alone qualifies as our Saviour.

So it is that, while inviting all to come to Christ, the New Testament is exclusivist in that it is clear that it is only in Christ that salvation can be found (John 3:16-18, 36).

Faith alone?

Many people would like to think that sincere people who follow other religions or none will also be saved even if they do not trust personally in Christ. C. S. Lewis promotes this idea in the final book of the Chronicles of Narnia, *The Last Battle*. But we have to disagree with Lewis at this pont. That is to believe that people are saved by their sincerity rather than by faith in Christ and his work.

The Bible spells out that personal faith in Christ is necessary to be saved.

The teaching of Jesus

For God so loved the world that he gave his one and only Son, that whoever believes in him shall not perish but have eternal life. [17]For God did not send his Son into the world to condemn the world, but to save the world through him. [18]Whoever believes in him is not condemned, but whoever does not believe stands condemned already because he has not believed in the name of God's one and only Son. (John 3:16-18)

[44]He said to them, 'This is what I told you while I was still with you: Everything must be fulfilled that is written about me in the Law of Moses, the Prophets and the Psalms.' [45]Then he opened their minds so they could understand the Scriptures. [46]He told them, 'This is what is written: The Christ will suffer and rise from the dead on the third day, [47]and repentance and forgiveness of sins will be preached in his name to all nations, beginning at Jerusalem. [48]You are witnesses of these things. [49]I am going to send you what my Father has promised; but stay in the city until you have been clothed with power from on high.' (Luke 24:44-49)

Jesus declares that the nations need to hear, repent and believe in him to be saved. Look at Luke 24:44-49. Here we see four things:

- The current condition of people is that they need forgiveness (verse 47) – as they are, they are not forgiven.
- They must repent (verse 47).

- What must be provided for them in order to repent? A proclamation (verses 46-47) of the name of Christ and his death and resurrection.
- How many people are in this condition and need such a proclamation? All nations (verse 47). The conclusion must be that there is no forgiveness apart from hearing of and turning to Christ.

The teaching of Paul

[16]I am not ashamed of the gospel, because it is the power of God for the salvation of everyone who believes: first for the Jew, then for the Gentile. [17]For in the gospel a righteousness from God is revealed, a righteousness that is by faith from first to last, just as it is written: 'The righteous will live by faith.' (Rom. 1:16-17)

What shall we conclude then? Are we any better? Not at all! We have already made the charge that Jews and Gentiles are all under sin...[19]Now we know that whatever the law says, it says to those who are under the law, so that every mouth may be silenced and the whole world held accountable to God. [20]Therefore no one will be declared righteous in his sight by observing the law; rather, through the law we become conscious of sin. [21]But now a righteousness from God, apart from law, has been made known, to which the Law and the Prophets testify. [22]This righteousness from God comes through faith in Jesus Christ to all who believe. There is no difference, [23]for all have sinned and fall short of the glory of God, [24]and are justified freely by his grace through the redemption that came by Christ Jesus. [25]God presented him as a sacrifice of atonement, through faith in his blood. He did this to demonstrate his justice, because in his forbearance he had left the sins committed beforehand unpunished— [26]he did it to demonstrate his justice at the present time, so as to be just and the one who justifies those who have faith in Jesus. (Rom. 3:9, 19-26)

[1]Brothers, my heart's desire and prayer to God for the Israelites is that they may be saved. [2]For I can testify about them that they are zealous for God, but their zeal is not based on knowledge. [3]Since they did not know the righteousness that comes from God and sought to establish their own, they did not submit to God's righteousness. [4]Christ is the end of the law so that there may be righteousness for everyone who believes. (Rom. 10:1-4)

Look at Romans 1:16-17, the first passage quoted above. Notice that the gospel is the power of God for the salvation 'of everyone who believes'. Paul is quite explicit that faith is necessary. Some people try to get around this by saying that this is just a general faith in God. But that cannot be, because the Jews (for example) did have a faith in God; yet still Paul insists (with tears) that though many of them are zealous and sincere, they are lost apart from turning to Christ (Rom. 10:1-4, the last passage quoted). The faith required is faith in Christ.

The story of Cornelius
[1]At Caesarea there was a man named Cornelius, a centurion in what was known as the Italian Regiment. [2]He and all his family were devout and God-fearing; he gave generously to those in need and prayed to God regularly. [3]One day at about three in the afternoon he had a vision. He distinctly saw an angel of God, who

came to him and said, 'Cornelius!' [4]Cornelius stared at him in fear. 'What is it, Lord?' he asked. The angel answered, 'Your prayers and gifts to the poor have come up as a memorial offering before God. [5]Now send men to Joppa to bring back a man named Simon who is called Peter. [6]He is staying with Simon the tanner, whose house is by the sea.' [7]When the angel who spoke to him had gone, Cornelius called two of his servants and a devout soldier who was one of his attendants. [8]He told them everything that had happened and sent them to Joppa. [9]About noon the following day as they were on their journey and approaching the city, Peter went up on the roof to pray. [10]He became hungry and wanted something to eat, and while the meal was being prepared, he fell into a trance. [11]He saw heaven opened and something like a large sheet being let down to earth by its four corners. [12]It contained all kinds of four-footed animals, as well as reptiles of the earth and birds of the air. [13]Then a voice told him, 'Get up, Peter. Kill and eat.' [14]'Surely not, Lord!' Peter replied. 'I have never eaten anything impure or unclean.' [15]The voice spoke to him a second time, 'Do not call anything impure that God has made clean.' [16]This happened three times, and immediately the sheet was taken back to heaven. [17]While Peter was wondering about the meaning of the vision, the men sent by Cornelius found out where Simon's house was and stopped at the gate. [18]They called out, asking if Simon who was known as Peter was staying there. [19]While Peter was still thinking about the vision, the Spirit said to him, 'Simon, three men are looking for you. [20]So get up and go downstairs. Do not hesitate to go with them, for I have sent them.' [21]Peter went down and said to the men, 'I'm the one you're looking for. Why have you come?' [22]The men replied, 'We have come from Cornelius the centurion. He is a righteous and God-fearing man, who is respected by all the Jewish people. A holy angel told him to have you come to his house so that he could hear what you have to say.' [23]Then Peter invited the men into the house to be his guests. The next day Peter started out with them, and some of the brothers from Joppa went along. [24]The following day he arrived in Caesarea. Cornelius was expecting them and had called together his relatives and close friends. [25]As Peter entered the house, Cornelius met him and fell at his feet in reverence. [26]But Peter made him get up. 'Stand up,' he said, 'I am only a man myself.' [27]Talking with him, Peter went inside and found a large gathering of people. [28]He said to them: 'You are well aware that it is against our law for a Jew to associate with a Gentile or visit him. But God has shown me that I should not call any man impure or unclean. [29]So when I was sent for, I came without raising any objection. May I ask why you sent for me?' [30]Cornelius answered: 'Four days ago I was in my house praying at this hour, at three in the afternoon. Suddenly a man in shining clothes stood before me [31]and said, "Cornelius, God has heard your prayer and remembered your gifts to the poor. [32]Send to Joppa for Simon who is called Peter. He is a guest in the home of Simon the tanner, who lives by the sea." [33]So I sent for you immediately, and it was good of you to come. Now we are all here in the presence of God to listen to everything the Lord has commanded you to tell us.' [34]Then Peter began to speak: 'I now realize how true it is that God does not show favouritism [35]but accepts men from every nation who fear him and do what is right. [36]You know the message God sent to the people of Israel, telling the good news of peace through Jesus Christ, who is Lord of all. [37]You know what has happened throughout Judea, beginning in Galilee after the baptism that John preached— [38]how God anointed Jesus of Nazareth with the Holy Spirit and power, and how he went around doing good and healing all who were under the power of the devil, because God was with him.   [39]'We are witnesses of everything he did in the country of the Jews and in Jerusalem. They killed him by hanging him on a tree, [40]but God raised him from the dead on the third day and caused him to be seen. [41]He was not seen by all the people, but by witnesses whom God had already chosen—by us who ate and drank with him after he rose from the dead. [42]He commanded us to preach to the people and to testify that he is the one whom God appointed as judge of the living and the dead. [43]All the prophets testify about him that everyone who believes in him receives forgiveness of sins through his name.' [44]While Peter was still speaking these words, the Holy Spirit came on all who heard the message. [45]The circumcised believers who had come with Peter were astonished that the gift of the Holy Spirit had been poured out even on the Gentiles. [46]For they heard them speaking in tongues and praising God. Then Peter said, [47]'Can anyone keep these people from being baptized with water? They have received the Holy Spirit just as we have.' [48]So he ordered that they be baptized in the name of Jesus Christ. Then they asked Peter to stay with them for a few days.

[1]The apostles and the brothers throughout Judea heard that the Gentiles also had received the word of God. [2]So when Peter went up to Jerusalem, the circumcised

believers criticized him [3]and said, 'You went into the house of uncircumcised men and ate with them.' [4]Peter began and explained everything to them precisely as it had happened: [5]'I was in the city of Joppa praying, and in a trance I saw a vision. I saw something like a large sheet being let down from heaven by its four corners, and it came down to where I was. [6]I looked into it and saw four-footed animals of the earth, wild beasts, reptiles, and birds of the air. [7]Then I heard a voice telling me, "Get up, Peter. Kill and eat." [8]I replied, "Surely not, Lord! Nothing impure or unclean has ever entered my mouth." [9]The voice spoke from heaven a second time, "Do not call anything impure that God has made clean." [10]This happened three times, and then it was all pulled up to heaven again. [11]Right then three men who had been sent to me from Caesarea stopped at the house where I was staying. [12]The Spirit told me to have no hesitation about going with them. These six brothers also went with me, and we entered the man's house. [13]He told us how he had seen an angel appear in his house and say, "Send to Joppa for Simon who is called Peter. [14]He will bring you a message through which you and all your household will be saved." [15]As I began to speak, the Holy Spirit came on them as he had come on us at the beginning. [16]Then I remembered what the Lord had said: "John baptized with water, but you will be baptized with the Holy Spirit." [17]So if God gave them the same gift as he gave us, who believed in the Lord Jesus Christ, who was I to think that I could oppose God?' [18]When they heard this, they had no further objections and praised God, saying, 'So then, God has granted even the Gentiles repentance unto life.'

We are told at the beginning that Cornelius is a very sincere and pious man (10:1-2). And yet God sends an angel to tell him to send for Peter, because he still needs to hear the gospel in order to be saved. God's plans no longer favour just one nation, the Jews (10:35). Peter tells Cornelius that all who believe in him (the one who has been raised from the dead, 10:40) will be saved (10:43). It was through the message that Peter brings, Cornelius was told, that he and he house would be saved (11:14) – the implication is that he was not saved beforehand. The conclusion is that pious non-Christians need the gospel.

There is only one cure for sin – Christ. And we take that medicine through faith. All the world is infected with the same disease of sin. Therefore all the world needs the same cure.

Those who have never heard of Jesus?

Good Christians struggle over the question, 'What about those who have never heard?' It is a poignant question, but there are three things to bear in mind.

First, God is just, and he will deal justly with those who have never heard. *Second*, the fact that there are people who have never heard should cause us to redouble our efforts to make sure they do hear. Romans 10:14 spurs us on to evangelism when it asks concerning unbelievers, 'How can they believe in the one of whom they have not heard? And how can they hear without someone preaching to them?' But *thirdly*, we must not think that any one of us ever 'deserved' to hear the gospel. Our sins are such that none of us deserve anything from God. So it is not a matter of God's injustice if people do not hear. Beware of trying to put God on trial or accusing him in this way.

Our job is to accept the Bible's simple teaching that Christ is the Saviour and personal faith in him is necessary for salvation.

The gospel in a PC world

Obviously, the exclusivity of the gospel is very objectionable to people who have imbibed the outlook of political correctness. Indeed, the message of the cross always to some extent causes offence to sinners, speaking as it does of sin, the judgement of God and the one way of salvation.

However, we must be careful not to add unnecessarily to the offence of the cross by our attitudes in the way we bring the good news to others.

We are not saying that others must turn to Christ because we say so, but because God says so. If they ask how we know God says so, we must humbly try to show them the reasons why we believe truth is not a matter of opinion, why the Bible can be relied upon, and why the gospel is actually true. However, ultimately, because the god of this world has blinded people's eyes, we will face much prejudice which only the Holy Spirit's power can overcome.

(I am very indebted to two lectures by Dr Bruce Ware of Southern Baptist Seminary, Louisville, Kentucky, which he gave at the Carey Conference of 2007. My notes from those two lectures are the basis of this chapter.)

Chapter 9
Where has feminism taken us?

Secular society increasingly expects women to be in paid work. In particular, to think in old-fashioned terms that a mother's place should be primarily in the home is frowned upon. This is most definitely politically incorrect. Here we seek to think through some of the issues involved in this for Christian women.

We will first of all try to give a description of both what the Bible has to say about women in the work-place and the changes that have come about in society in this area.

Biblical Basics on Gender

The Bible makes it quite clear that men and women are equal, both made in the image of God (Gen.1:27), together to lovingly rule over and cultivate the potentials of God's world (Gen. 1:28). The two genders are complementary. Men are to seek to provide Christ-like headship, expressed in protecting, providing and leading. They are to do this not with themselves and their benefit in view, but with the benefit of their wives and families uppermost (Eph. 5:25). Women have been created with a 'helper design' (Gen.2:18), sensitive and supporting towards others. All this is seen in the wider context of husband and wife serving the Lord together.

Thus, though allowances must be made for different types of personality, nevertheless, nurturing and relational abilities are central to true femininity. For the married mother, this means that her role as homemaker must have primary place in her priorities. But whether married or single, Christian women are to be 'mothers' using their female strengths to encourage others, and serve the Lord (1 Cor. 7:34). Even the apostle Paul speaks of the benefit he enjoyed through being 'mothered' by a woman who was not his mother (Rom. 16:13).

Our Changing Society

During the last century, especially under the exigencies of the two world wars and through the rise of feminism, the place of women in society has changed considerably.

- Women have been liberated from the assumption that they must *only* stay at home and look after the family. This restrictive attitude, which prohibited women from entering the work-place, was never a balanced Biblical attitude (Prov. 31:16, 18, 24; Acts 16:14).

- With increased life expectancy and the availability of contraception, most Western women today spend a far shorter proportion of their life in bearing and rearing children. Rightly, many want to put the abilities God has given them to good use in the church, the community or the work-place (Rom. 16:1; Acts 9:36).

- Many women *have* to get paid employment outside the home. Christian women who are single also usually have to support themselves. Christian women who are single mothers, divorcees or widows have little choice but to work full-time alongside looking after their families (Ruth 2:2). Such women often need special encouragement and support from the church (James 1:27).

Needed Safeguards

While the idea of women being involved in the work-place is very much a viable possibility in Scripture, nevertheless we have to reflect that Scripture would also bring certain safeguards to bear. It is possible to go too far along this line.

- *The primacy of family life.* A Biblical understanding of family and femininity implies that wives and mothers should not neglect the family for work. This matches the instincts of most women (Isa.49:15). A BBC TV *Panorama* programme in January 2000 reported research into 560 mothers who had begun full-time jobs. After two years, a third of the women had either left work or had taken part-time jobs. Many who remained in full-time employment wished they did not have to do so. They were dissatisfied with having to leave their children with child-minders.

- *Self-worth and ambition.* Success at work is almost crucial to men's self-confidence. The problem is that feminism has identified this male goal as the ideal for women too, denying the essential differences between men and women. 'The idea that women may value other aspects of life more highly than earning money is dismissed as preposterous. So, of course, if women aren't working, they can't possibly have chosen not to. Yet this is usually precisely the case' (Melanie Phillips, *Sex Change Society*). The Bible commends industry and condemns laziness (Prov. 31:27); but ambition needs to be focused on living to help others and glorify God, not on worldly wealth or prestige (Luke 12:18-20). True self-worth comes not from our supposed achievements, but from finding ourselves the objects of God's love and through Christ being adopted into his family.

- *Sexual temptation and harassment.* It is foolish and naïve to ignore the fact that women are not only attractive, but relatively speaking are physically weaker (1 Peter 3:7), and thus vulnerable to men. Care needs to be taken in this area. Modesty of dress is essential. A good employer will seek to protect women at work, and good women will show a willingness to accept such care (Ruth 2:8-14). Women themselves can also be tempted.

- *Equal Opportunities.* Christians ought to be concerned for justice (Micah 6:8; Matt. 7:12); but we must be careful to base our views on facts, not misinformation. Research shows that women across Europe divide into three camps. About 20% are totally home-centred and prefer not to have paid employment. Another 20% are work-centred, either remaining childless or having children looked after by others. By far the greatest proportion, about 60%, want to combine work and family in some way. 'The assumption of British policy makers, which seems to be that all women want to work and all that stands in their way is affordable childcare, is simply wrong' (Melanie Phillips). While Christians ought to support the justice of 'equal opportunities' (Prov. 1:3, Luke 18:5), in terms of giving women the choice to enter the work-place, it is totally unrealistic to expect 'equal outcomes' in terms of 50% of every profession being female. This ignores the preference that the majority of women have to make time for their families. It is disingenuous to argue that discrimination is going on when so many women genuinely prefer to stay at home to care for their families, or else to work part time. According to recent statistics, childless married women, single career women and men actually earn much the same.

Women's strengths in the work-place

In the 1970s and 80s it was thought that a woman had to 'become a man' in order to succeed at work. The idea was that they had to become single-minded and ruthless. But time has shown that to be untrue. Women can bring a uniquely helpful dimension. The particular strengths of a Biblical femininity come in such areas as communication (Prov. 31:26), empathy (1 Sam. 25:23-25) and nurturing teamwork rather than competition between colleagues.

Reflecting the complementary purposes for which God made us, the brains of men and women are 'wired' differently. This means that whereas the male brain is more focused and compartmentalised, the female brain is far better at coping with handling many different tasks at once. It is interesting to count the many tasks in which the woman of Proverbs 31 is engaged at once. Thus a woman's influence can bring more integration to a work-place.

'The stereotype of exaggerated femininity is that women are prone to act on impulse, guided by feeling, and sometimes hasty in words. Maturity enables a woman to temper such instincts: to act on principles not impulse…But a wise woman will carefully utilise, rather than ignore her intuitions and feelings. By doing so she will be contributing a positive, warm factor to what otherwise might be a rather clinically objective working environment' (Sharon James, *Roles without Relegation*).

Problems with the current situation

The Biblical approach to gender allows for much flexibility but, for married people, it does see the work-place as the primary focus for the man and the home as the primary focus for the woman. This is what we have tried to point out previously in this chapter.

However, this position is deemed 'not politically correct'. It is regarded as a threat to 'equality'. The outlook which is pressed upon us by the media and the government is that the work-place ought to be the primary focus for both genders. This attitude is betrayed in the way we now speak of women as taking 'a career break' to have children, and by governments headlining their efforts to provide childcare at an ever-lower age so that women can get back to work as soon as possible.

Moving away from the Biblical model is seen as 'progress' for women and for society. Yet, though we must still wait to see how things will finally pan out from the rise of this feminist approach, there are definite signs that problems are accruing. Let me mention three as we close this chapter.

- *The first is financial.* The last fifty years have seen women directed into careers and into the work-place. At the same time we have seen in Britain a tremendous increase in the cost of living, and in particular in the cost of buying a house. From our own experience, the price of a house has increased 10-fold or more in the last thirty years. Obviously, there are many factors which have come together to bring about this increase. But one factor is certainly the increased earning power of women. It used to be that a married man's salary alone paid the mortgage. As more and more couples had two wages, as both husband and wife went to work, it meant that they could afford to pay a bigger mortgage. But given a limited housing stock and the way that the market works, the overall outcome of this has simply been that houses went up in price. Market economics mean that the price of a house settles at what most couples can afford. Now, with two incomes, the average couple can afford more; and the house costs more. There are all kinds of ramifications to this. Married women who would like to choose to stay at home with the children find that they cannot afford to do so. The mortgage needs to be paid, and a husband rarely earns enough to do this on his own. Single people and especially single mothers are often priced out of the housing market. Whether it is true or not, I do not know; but some people suspect that feminism has actually been promoted by governments in quite a cynical way. Under the old system, each family generally had only one wage earner and therefore only one person paying income tax. Now, in the new 'politically correct' situation, there are two people earning and two people to tax. More goes to the government coffers.

- *The second is familial.* All women, including mothers, are encouraged to have a career and to enter the work-place. But who is to look after the children? Obviously things are not quite so difficult once the children go to school. But that is not until around the age of five. The government has gone out of its way to encourage nursery schools and child-minding – even for quite young children. But what effect does that have on the child and his or her development? The government has given the impression that such arrangements are fine. Few psychologists have this opinion. In his book *Affluenza*, the clinical child psychologist and broadcaster Oliver James has written the following: 'The available evidence on the effects of non-maternal, substitute care before the age of three is highly controversial. The most reliable review concluded that 41% of babies or toddlers (under 3 years old) cared for by someone other than their mother (or father) for more than 20 hours a week are insecure, whereas this is true of 26% of children cared for exclusively by mothers. Further evidence has consistently revealed higher levels of aggression and hyperactivity in day-cared children, still evident at the age of seven.' Obviously, there are caveats which go with this evidence. For example, the quality of the child's relationship with its parents before entering day-care, will very much help the child. Nevertheless, the idea that for a youngster to be child-minded is just as good as being with his or her parent is questionable.

- *The third is psychological.* As women have been persuaded that they must aim at a career in the work-place, there has been an increasing concern that girls should do well at school. Better exam results lead to better job prospects. The exam success of many girls, overtaking the boys, has been much trumpeted by the politically correct media. Once again, listen to psychologist Oliver James. 'You might suppose that their greater freedoms and higher achievements would be good for their well-being. In fact a study published in 2003 reveals the opposite. The study looked at levels of anxiety and depression in two very large (5,000 plus) representative samples of 15-year-olds, one in 1987 and the other in 1999. Amongst the bottom social class, girls' rates rose only a little, but in the top class, the rise was 24% in 1987 to a startling 38% in 1999 – more than one-third of the most privileged and successful. Contrary to popular perceptions of teenage male emotional apocalypse, there was no significant increase in problems amongst the boys, but for the girls, rates of the kind of distress that can cause hospitalisation rose 3-fold (from 6% to 18%). The period between 1987 and 1999 was one in which girls began to outperform boys in almost every academic subject at every educational stage. In 1987 there was virtually no difference in how well the genders did at GCSE, but by 1999 a gap had opened: whereas 43% of boys got 5 or more at grades A to C, 53% of girls did so. This greater success of the girls precisely mirrors their increased emotional distress. ..The excellent academic performance of high-income girls correlated with ill-being.' Again, these statistics can be challenged and perhaps there are other explanations of this correlation. But as we see pressure to be successful going alongside young girls with eating disorders and other psychological problems, one is again caused to ask whether we are on the right road.

To these three problems we could add many more. But the problems highlighted do serve to raise a pertinent question. Where has feminism got us? Though there have undoubtedly been some changes for the good, has our world become too dogmatic in our approach to the sexes? In doggedly pursuing the politically correct agenda of treating male and female as if they were the same, are we actually causing more harm than good?

Recommended reading:

James Tooley, *The Mis-education of Women* (London: Continuum, 2002)

Chapter 10
Evangelicalism falling for it?

If the ship is in the sea, that is fine. But if the sea is in the ship, that means trouble. And it is likely to be big trouble. Similarly, if the church is in the world, that is as it should be, reaching out to the lost and needy. But if the world is in the church, the church is facing catastrophe.

Under the pressures of the post-modern PC world, evangelical churches have begun to change. There is a sense in which some change is necessary and inevitable as the culture in which the church operates changes. Just as we would expect a missionary from the West to seek to understand African thinking or adapt to Asian ways in order to get alongside the people and be able to express the gospel in the most appropriate ways for the people he or she is seeking to reach, so we expect the church to change as the surrounding culture in the West changes.

However, what must not change is the gospel itself. We are prepared to change in order to communicate the unchangeable gospel. Paul's great adaptable strategy for sharing the good news expressed in 1 Corinthians 9:19-23 is well known.

> [19]Though I am free and belong to no man, I make myself a slave to everyone, to win as many as possible. [20]To the Jews I became like a Jew, to win the Jews. To

those under the law I became like one under the law (though I myself am not under the law), so as to win those under the law. [21]To those not having the law I became like one not having the law (though I am not free from God's law but am under Christ's law), so as to win those not having the law. [22]To the weak I became weak, to win the weak. I have become all things to all men so that by all possible means I might save some. [23]I do all this for the sake of the gospel, that I may share in its blessings.

But, sadly, unlike Paul, there are indications that in adapting to post-modern, therapy culture in a PC world, many churches are losing matters which are central to the gospel or vital to a proper expression of the gospel. They are not simply altering their style, they are altering the content of the gospel and what they stand for. There are attempts to change things which should never be changed.

In this chapter we explore this subject by looking at a couple of books which have been popular in the Christian world in recent years, yet which actually, under the pressures of the current PC outlook, have (in my view) totally betrayed the Biblical gospel. These books are *The Shack,* a novel by William Paul Young, first published in 2007, and *Love Wins,* a more didactic book by Rob Bell from a background of the 'emerging church', published in 2011. As we review these books and think about what they are saying, we will see how they change the great doctrines of Scripture and truths central to the gospel in order to curry favour with our PC world and its therapy culture.

The Shack: Re-inventing God

The Shack is a best-selling novel which tries to address the question of suffering. It is not just a fictional tale but a theological tract promoting the author's ideas. It has proved enormously popular in some Christian circles.

As with all things, we test its teaching by the Bible (1 Thess. 5:21; 2 Tim. 3:16).

The Shack is a story, set in the United States, that revolves around Mack (Mackenzie) Philips. Four years before the story begins, Mack's young daughter, Missy, was abducted during a family holiday and brutally murdered in an isolated shack by a notorious serial killer. As the story begins, Mack, who has been living in the shadow of his 'Great Sadness' receives a note from God (known in this story as Papa). Papa invites Mack to return to this shack to meet up. Mack visits the scene of the crime and there experiences a weekend-long encounter with God.

Each of the members of the Trinity is present and each appears in bodily form. The Father, Papa, whose actual name is Elousia (which is Greek for *tenderness*) appears in the form of a large, matronly African-American woman (though near the book's end, because Mack requires a father figure, she turns into a pony-tailed, grey-haired man). Jesus is a young to middle-aged man of Middle-Eastern descent, while the Holy Spirit is played by Sarayu (Sanskrit for *air* or *wind*), a small Asian woman. The reader learns that Mack has been given this opportunity to meet with God so that he could learn to deal with the overwhelming pain and anger resulting from the death of his daughter.

153

As the weekend progresses, Mack participates in lengthy discussions with each member of the Trinity. Topics range from the cross to the Trinity and from forgiveness to free will. He finds his understanding of God and his relationship with God radically altered. As we might expect, he leaves the shack greatly changed. The main point to keep in mind, however, is that Mack is a hurt person, a victim. The politically correct outlook and therapy culture with which we live encourages us all to see ourselves as victims. This is the way the connection to the reader is meant to be facilitated.

There are two positive aspects of the book. *First*, it is a book which takes seriously the depth of human suffering and seeks to show great compassion. *Second*, it rightly tells us that our deepest sufferings and heartaches can ultimately only be helped and healed through encountering and knowing God personally (Isa. 61:1; Matt. 11:28; 2 Cor. 12:7-10; Rev. 21:1-4).

However, apart from this, there are so many problems with *The Shack* that it is actually a very dangerous book which needs to be handled with great discernment. It is in fact a rewriting of the gospel and a re-imagining of God to suit the victim mindset and therapy culture of our day.

A Manipulative Book

First of all (remember this is a work of fiction), the author pulls out all the stops to get the reader firmly on the side of his hero Mack and against the ordinary evangelical church. This is set up in the first few pages as we are told that Mack's father was an overly strict church elder with a secret drink problem, and who beat his wife. As a distressed youngster, Mack shares this with another church leader. The leader tells his father and

Mack is so mercilessly beaten 'with a belt and Bible verses' that he leaves home.

By this device, the reader has already been given a negative view of the church and the Bible. A platform is being set up on which the author will go on to build. Church is 'endless meetings staring at the backs of people's heads'. The Bible is God's voice reduced to paper only understandable by experts, which produces 'a stoic and unfeeling faith'. So readers are being manoeuvred to set aside the church and Scripture as their guides and are laid open to accepting the author's ideas. This, of course, is intensified as our sympathy is aroused towards Mack because of the great tragedy he has suffered in the murder of his daughter.

There are two points to make here.

• Mack is wanting to know God more directly, and Bible faith is dismissed as not enough. Our therapy culture wants comfort now. We want to feel good now. But Christianity is about faith now and seeing God in the future (Matt. 5:8). The book gets the balance between the *already* and *not yet* of God's kingdom wrong (Rom. 8:18). It suffers from an over-realised eschatology. Here we live by faith in God's promises.

• The ploy of grabbing our emotions, with sympathy for Mack, before addressing our thinking is a classic move of false teachers. The Puritan William Gurnall likens them to adulterers seeking to seduce a woman. 'Indeed it would be hard work for the adulterer to convince her he would prostitute, that the act is lawful; no, he goes another way to work. First, by some amorous insinuations he inveigles her affections, and they, once bewitched, the other is not much questioned' (*The Christian in Complete Armour*).

An Heretical Book

Sadly, we have to say that the book teaches terrible heresy. *The Shack* promotes false teaching in three crucial areas of Christian doctrine. Here is a brief sketch of some of the problems.

The doctrine of revelation

How has God or does God reveal himself to us? The answer of Scripture is that though God has given a revelation of himself in creation which leaves men without excuse before him, this revelation cannot bring salvation (Rom. 1:18-21; 2:14-15). For this reason it pleased God, through the Holy Spirit, to give us the Scriptures of the Old and New Testaments, which lead us to faith in his Son, Christ the Saviour (2 Tim. 3:15). Yet consistently *The Shack* plays down the place of the Bible and replaces it with personal experience. This is classic. It adopts the therapy culture, experience-centred, emotional take on life. In the novel, God says 'You might see me in a piece of art, or music, or silence, or through people, or in Creation, or in your joy and sorrow.'

The doctrine of salvation

Though the cross is central to Scripture, with the four Gospels majoring on Christ's sacrifice, it appears only sparingly in *The Shack*. The reason for this is that the book does not believe in a holy God for whom sin is a problem. William Paul Young has God saying, 'I don't need to punish people for sin. Sin is its own punishment, devouring you from the inside. It's not my purpose to punish it; it's my joy to cure it.' This is a 'God'

156

invented for the needs of our therapeutic age, not the true holy God of Scripture (Rom. 1:18; 2 Thess. 1:8). Once again it has bought into the cultural shift from a moral outlook to the priority of what is emotionally attractive to contemporary Westerners. Sin is a moral problem, our biggest problem before a holy God. But that will not do for today's world. So *The Shack* simply ditches it. It rewrites the gospel to suit the preferences of present society.

A person unfamiliar with the Bible will not be able to glean any Biblical understanding of what it means that 'Christ died for our sins' and rose again on the third day (1 Cor.15:3-4; 2 Cor. 5:21; Gal.3:13). Further, according to *The Shack*, becoming a Christian and having personal faith in Christ is unnecessary for salvation. In the book, 'Jesus' is quoted as saying, 'I have no desire to make them Christian, but I do want to join them in their transformation into sons and daughters of my Papa, into my brothers and sisters, into my Beloved.' In an attempt to tick the politically correct box of 'inclusiveness' the classical mission of the church is dismissed. The Great Commission is rendered redundant.

The doctrine of the Trinity

The Bible tells us of the Father, 'No one has ever seen God, but God the One and Only, who is at the Father's side, has made him known' (John 1:18). Jesus is the true image of God (Heb. 1:3) and to dream up other representations of the Father is blasphemous (Rom. 1:22-23; 1 Tim. 2:5).

The Biblical doctrine of the Trinity is a mystery, but can be succinctly stated as follows: 'God is three Persons, Father, Son and Holy Spirit. Each Person is fully God. There is one God.'

There are five areas concerning the Trinity which *The Shack* denies.

- *First*, there is order in the Trinity. In both creation and redemption, the Father has authority, the Son obeys and submits, and the Spirit submits to both and glorifies the Son who glorifies the Father. Scripture specifically says that the Father is the head of the Son (1 Cor. 11:3; John 6:38; 8:28). This in no way makes the Son less God than the Father, any more than the husband being the head of the wife (Eph.5:23) makes her less human than her husband. But *The Shack* is specifically against all authority within relationships. In the novel we read, 'Mackenzie, we have no concept of final authority among us, only unity. We are in a circle of relationship, not a chain of command.' One suspects that the concept of authority is rejected because in the politically correct milieu of the victim mindset authority is always misused.

- *Second*, there is distinction within the Trinity. For example, though the Son became incarnate, this is impossible for the Father (1 Tim. 6:15-16). Yet *The Shack* continually seeks to blur the distinctions, so that (for example) the 'Father' (Papa) has the scars of crucifixion, as if all three Persons were crucified. Again, unless all three Persons are somehow crucified, it might look as if Jesus was a victim and the Father not. This would not do in our PC world.

- *Third*, there the matter of identity. *The Shack* chooses to portray God as feminine. This is straight surrender to politically correctness again. But God has chosen to reveal himself to us as masculine (Luke 11:2; Ps. 40:2; 46:9, etc.) and gives us no leeway to re-imagine him as female or anything else.

- *Fourth*, we must protect the Personhood of God. William Young, the author, plays around with the idea of the Unitarian–Universalist Buckminster Fuller and has God saying of himself 'I am a verb, I am that I am.' But a verb is what someone does, and so is less than a person. This reduces God to a kind of force. It is a terrible parody of God's identity revealed to Moses in Exodus 3:14, 'I AM WHO I AM.'

- *Fifth*, we must be concerned for the glory of God. In Scripture, when someone meets God face to face, or when Jesus reveals his glory, people fall down, overwhelmed with awe. In this novel, Mack has no such sense of worship in God's presence, but rather is prepared to use foul language (see pages 140, 224). Rather, his encounter with God is just like hanging out for a while with an old buddy.

We must conclude that the 'God' of *The Shack* is not the God of the Bible and that God has been 're-imagined' to curry favour with the mindset of a world which the Bible tells us is in rebellion against God (Rom. 8.7-8).

An Unnecessary Book

The fictional scenario of *The Shack* is paralleled by the true story of Job in the Bible. Job is a man who has suffered terrible tragedy, including the death not of one, but ten children. You do not have to write a fiction like *The Shack* to plumb the depths of human suffering. These things are addressed face on in Scripture.

Afflicted with a diseased body and in an agony of soul, Job longs to meet with God (Job 23:3). In fact, many of the great

159

questions which come from Job in his suffering are answered by Jesus (see Job 14:14 / John 11:25; Job 23:3 / John 14:9; Job 9:33 / 1 Tim. 2:5). The book of Job, of course, tells us that it is Satan, not God, who afflicts Job, although God allows it. Job refuses to curse God and finally, at the end of the book, God appears to him in a great whirlwind and Job finds himself both overwhelmed, exonerated and doubly rewarded and restored. The book of Job gives a much more thorough and nuanced approach to the problem of pain without distorting God's holy character or relinquishing God's authority or sovereignty over the world.

Books like *The Shack* become popular because they scratch where people itch. We live in a culture which encourages people to see themselves as casualties, as hard-done-by. There must be a lot of Christians out there who are in pain and have bought into victimhood and therapy culture. The answer to their difficulties is not the wonky theology of *The Shack* but the Biblical theology of the love of a sovereign and therefore reliable God who promises us eternal life, with no more suffering, through his Son Jesus, who suffered for us.

Let us now turn to reviewing a second very influential book.

Love Wins: the attack on John 3:16

This controversial book by American Rob Bell burst upon the scene in 2011 and for a whole weekend became the most talked-about topic on the internet in the United States.

The book is actually a sustained attack on the idea that those who fail to trust in Jesus Christ in this life are lost eternally because of their sins. Put like that, you can see that the book is an assault on Christianity itself, because traditionally all the denominations, Protestant and indeed Catholic, have believed this one way or another. They have believed John 3:16: 'For God so loved the world that he gave his one and only Son, that whoever believes in him shall not perish but have eternal life.'

Bell says that you do not necessarily need to believe; and in the end (probably) no one will perish. He calls traditional Christianity 'misguided and toxic'.

Two things might be thought surprising. *First*, this attack does not come from an ardent secularist but from someone who would call themselves a follower of Jesus. The *second* surprise is that quite a few people within the church want to embrace the book. Sadly, these surprises are not surprising at all. Let us see why. Once again it is to do with 'evangelicals' buying into the current Western world's preferred way of thinking.

Filling in the background

We must ask why Bell and other church leaders have become so uncomfortable with what traditional Christianity stands for; I am tempted to say 'ashamed' of the gospel (Rom.1.16; 2 Tim. 1.8). There are two aspects here.

Contemporary secular culture

The apostles warn us that the church must beware of being too affected by the worldly culture in which it lives (e.g. Rom.12:2). As I have tried to point out in this book, during the last century, with the increase of secularism, Western society has moved from a moral culture to a culture of emotion. Good is no longer defined in moral terms. Without God we are not even sure what morality is. Good is now generally what 'feels good'. There is no other point to life except enjoying yourself. Whereas fifty years ago even ordinary secular people would say that their aim in life was to be 'decent' people, now the goal of life is 'to be fulfilled; to enjoy myself'. And moving from a moral outlook to an emotional outlook makes people see things differently, just as a cricketer and a farmer might see a rain cloud in a totally different way. The cricketer frowns at the rain cloud because it might hinder his game. The farmer is thankful for the rain cloud as it will water his crops.

Today, people view things differently from the way they did fifty or sixty years ago. They no longer see through moral eyes, but through emotional spectacles. For example, when President Obama announced that special forces had finally killed the terrorist Osama bin Laden, you could almost feel the upset of some parts of the politically correct news media. That bin Laden gloried in the fact that he was behind the deaths of 3000 people on 9/11 and therefore morally deserved to die does not register.

We have lost that moral way of seeing things. But the moral view of the world was Jesus' view of the world. Mankind's central problem is a moral one; the problem of our sin. Jesus said, 'This is the verdict: Light has come into the world, but men loved darkness instead of light because their deeds were evil. Everyone who does evil hates the light, and will not come into the light for fear that his deeds will be exposed' (John 3:19-20).

The reason that Christianity is rejected in the West at present is not because the church is preaching the wrong message and needs to rewrite the gospel. People reject Christ and are lost because of moral failure which they do not want to acknowledge.

This does not go down well in the PC world driven by therapy culture. 'Feel good' finds that unacceptable. But the 'feel good' way of seeing things has rubbed off on many within the church. It has rubbed off on the author of *Love Wins*, Rob Bell, and hence he wants to rewrite Christianity's message.

The emergent church

Bell's background is in what has become known as 'the emergent church' (EMC). This is difficult to define, because its promoters would say that it is not a movement with cut and dried ideas, but a conversation (blogs, meetings, etc.) between Christians.

Uncomfortable with the 'arrogant certainty' of evangelicalism, EMC has bought into post-modernism. Generally, the ethos is that religious feelings are what matters. Spiritual experience trumps Biblical revelation. This was precisely the outlook which became the springboard for the old theological liberalism. For those involved in EMC, 'truth' is more about the journey than coming to any conclusions, and all kinds of methods are used by EMC leaders to move Christians to downplay propositional truth.

'Can human language really cope with explaining the infinite God?' 'It's about your relationship with Jesus, not knowing truths about him.' 'People only give you their interpretation of the Bible.' These are the kinds of ideas fired out from certain EMC leaders. And in *Love Wins* Bell uses a well-worn EMC ploy of posing false dilemmas in order to forward his thesis. Let me quote what he says about the cross of Christ. 'What

163

happened on the cross? Is it the end of the sacrificial system or a broken relationship that has been reconciled or a guilty defendant who's been set free or a battle that's been won or redeeming of something that's been lost? Which is it? Which perspective is the right one? Which metaphor is correct? Which explanation is true?' The reader is made to feel caught on the horns of a dilemma.

Actually those explanations and many more are all true – these are false dichotomies. But what is going on here is that the idea is being slipped into the reader's consciousness that what went on at the cross is so big and so mysterious that we can never grasp it and so we had better not insist that we have the truth about it. We are being moved away from holding firm conclusions. This is all very much the ethos of post-modernism.

But the logic Bell is using is false. You do not have to know everything about something to know what is true about it. To take a trivial example, I do not have to know the exact number of spectators at the football World Cup Final in South Africa in 2010 to know the fact that Spain won and they defeated the Netherlands 1 – 0. You do not have to know everything to know something. You do not have to know all truth to know truth. Yes, we may never be able to plumb the full depths of what happened at Calvary as the Son of God died for us, but that does not preclude us from being sure of the fact that at the cross, 'God so loved the world that he gave his one and only Son, that whoever believes in him shall not perish but have eternal life.'

But more importantly, this idea that we can never know the truth in a propositional way, which some EMC leaders would insist upon, is not Jesus' way of talking. Repeatedly, Jesus says to us, 'I tell you the truth' (e.g. John 3.3, 5). There is truth that is true for everyone. It is vital truth, about which we must not be vague, and which we must believe and act upon. Jesus said to Nicodemus, 'I tell you the truth, we speak of what we know, and we testify to what we have seen, but still you people do not accept our testimony' (John 3:11). God is quite capable of revealing himself and using human language to do so, and you cannot have a relationship with anyone (Jesus included) without knowing things that are true about them.

I may not know everything about how a lifeboat works but I know that if I jump into it I will be saved! And what evangelicals stand for is not 'arrogant certainty' but a humble passing on of what Jesus has said is true. But in a world which is inclusive and politically correct and likes the idea that 'all roads lead to God', Rob Bell wants to embrace more or less the same.

Nailing the specifics

As I say, it seems that *Love Wins* is a sustained attack on John 3:16. Let us pick out the key words to see what Bell is saying and ask whether he is right. Remember, that great Scripture verse says, 'For God so loved the world that he gave his one and only Son, that whoever believes in him shall not perish but have eternal life.'

The lost-ness of mankind (the world)

Much of what Bell says caricatures what evangelicals believe. As we shall see, the reason he is able to do this is that he assumes a basically secular / politically correct view of the world. He feels that the world is a bit lost. It does not have eternal life. But actually, people are not too bad. There is plenty of good out there. So he comes out with statements like, 'No hope for non-Christians? Is that what Jesus offers the world?' and 'Jesus is bigger than any one religion' (page 150). These words are very reminiscent of the 'equality of outcome' for all, regardless of life choices, which we saw in chapter 3 is so much a part of the politically correct view of things.

But that is not how Jesus sees the world. Yes, people may do relative good in their lives, but their 'good' is little more than rearranging the deck-chairs on the *Titanic*. Jesus sees the world as lost and in direst need. People are so lost that they require, not simply to turn over a new leaf, but to be thoroughly reborn. Jesus said, 'I tell you the truth, no one can see the kingdom of God unless he is born again' (John 3:3). He went on to say, 'I tell you the truth, no one can enter the kingdom of God unless he is born of water and the Spirit. Flesh gives birth to flesh, but the Spirit gives birth to spirit' (John 3:5-6). We are dying like those suffering from the bite of venomous snakes and need a miracle similar to the one which occurred for the rebellious children of Israel. Jesus explained, 'Just as Moses lifted up the snake in the desert, so the Son of Man must be lifted up, that everyone who believes in him may have eternal life' (John 3:14-15). The reason for this lost-ness is that we are sinners, as is exposed by our refusal to believe in God's Son. Of himself as God's Son, Jesus said, 'Whoever believes in him is not condemned, but whoever does not believe stands condemned already because he has not believed in the name of God's one and only Son' (John 3:18). What does that make other religions? Bell's view that there ought to be hope for non-Christians simply contradicts what Jesus says here. The only hope they have is to turn to Christ. Without Christ we are already condemned (John 3:18), and under God's wrath (John 3:36). That is the situation the gospel addresses.

The love of God (God so loved)

Here again Bell caricatures. He pictures a 'God' who loves you, but if you refuse to believe, when you die, he suddenly changes character and becomes your tormentor. 'Loving one moment, vicious the next. Kind and compassionate, only to become cruel and relentless in the blink of an eye' (page 174).

But that is not the God of the Bible. The God of the Bible does not change. But Bell is seeking to deflect responsibility away from people (responsibility does not go down well in therapy culture) and put it onto God. The true God is both incalculably holy and amazingly gracious; both at the same time. Because he is holy, he hates all sin and must condemn it. But because he is incredibly loving, he offers forgiveness and salvation to sinners. That is the dynamic of John 3:16. God *so loved*. What's that 'so' about? It expresses the unparalleled lengths to which God's love has gone. We are all self-centred rebels against God, most of us wishing either that he didn't exist at all or that if he does he ought to work for me! He ought to do what I tell him!

The real state of mankind was exposed by what we did to God's Son. 'This is the verdict: Light has come into the world, but men loved darkness instead of light because their deeds were evil' (John 3:19). But though such a world deserves nothing but God's total rejection, condemnation and wrath, God so loved that he gave his beloved Son to save us. From our verse it is not really clear who God loves the most, us or Jesus. God does not change. He does not delight in the death of a sinner. There is rejoicing in heaven when we are saved. He so loved.

The necessity of faith (whoever believes)

Once more Bell caricatures the gospel at this point of faith. 'So is it true,' he asks, 'that the kind of person you are doesn't ultimately matter, as long as you've said or prayed or believed the right things?' It's cheaply slanted to make the gospel look nasty.

But it is a deceit. *First*, no one says that faith which does not lead to a changed life saves you. So the bit about it not mattering what kind of person you are is a straw man. *Second*, the world's plane is already going down (because of our sins). Our good deeds will not lift the plane up again. Jesus is the parachute, the only way of escape for everyone; that is why faith is necessary. And *third*, Bell's words are calculated to make it look as though people are being kept out of heaven simply for not knowing the right password. But that is not it at all. Having been offered Christ, not to believe is to say, 'I don't want God's Son.' And that is what really tells you what kind of person you are. Jesus said, 'Everyone who does evil hates the light, and will not come into the light for fear that his deeds will be exposed. But whoever lives by the truth comes into the light, so that it may be seen plainly that what he has done has been done through God' (John 3:20-21).

The role of Christ (his one and only Son)

The cross, blood and sacrifice do not go down well in the warm, fuzzy world of our culture of emotion. 'Just the thought of such practices is repulsive. So primitive and barbaric. Not to mention unnecessary,' writes Rob Bell in *Love Wins*.

So he dismisses the New Testament version of the cross as sacrifice as just the way the apostles had of describing it in their cultural context where sacrifice was prevalent. So, he recommends, it is now time to change metaphors to suit our culture. With this in mind he comes up with a view of the cross which is not about atonement but about what he sees as a kind of universal truth that death brings life. You eat food: the plant has to die, but that gives you life. That is how the universe is. That is God's way, and that is what the cross of Jesus was showing us.

Actually, that is nonsense. Life does not come out of death. The only reason we can digest the plant is that we are alive already! Rob Bell's view is not Jesus' view. Yes, Jesus did use the picture of a seed dying to bring life when speaking of his death. But he operated in a Biblical world-view in which death is not natural, but the result of sin; and his death brings life only because it deals with our sin. Who is Jesus? He is 'the Lamb of God who takes away the sin of the world' (John 1:29). That is why God gave his one and only Son to death on the cross. It was so that 'whoever believes in him shall not perish but have eternal life' (John 3:16b).

The danger of hell (not perish)
Love Wins, the book is called. It cannot possibly be loving to punish sinners in hell forever. So Bell comes up with a kind of universalism in order to protect what he sees as God's tarnished reputation. And indeed man–centred political correctness does not like a God who judges us for our sin.

But just suppose that the love that really matters is not first of all God's love for us, but God's love for his Son, Jesus. This is brought to the fore in John's Gospel. The Father intends that all should honour the Son (John 5:23). This commitment is an expression of the eternal Father-Son relationship of love. Set against this backdrop, the everlasting rejection of the wicked becomes an expression of the intra-Trinitarian love between Father, Son and Holy Spirit rather than just a punishment for our sins.

Our sins and our clinging to them spring from our not wanting Christ. That is what is being said in John 3:19: 'This is the verdict: Light has come into the world, but men loved darkness instead of light because their deeds were evil.' And that is why 'Whoever believes in him is not condemned, but whoever does not believe is condemned already because he has not believed in the name of God's one and only Son' (John 3:18). God's wrath is an expression of a pure yet outraged love: it is the love of the Father for the Son that will not allow his Son's name to be belittled or despised. What Bell and those who reject hell are saying is, 'God has no right to love his Son that much!' But he does love him that much. And indeed, he loves you and me so much that he has given his Son so that we need not go to hell but may be forgiven and reconciled and included within God's love. He could not possibly love us more. But if we refuse, there is simply nowhere else for us to go without belittling Jesus; and that the Father will not do.

Meanwhile God's great offer is still on the table. 'For God so loved the world that he gave his one and only Son, that whoever believes in him shall not perish but have eternal life' (John 3:16).

Let me leave it there. I hope we have got the drift. I hope we have been able to see, as we have reviewed the contents of these best-selling books, *The Shack* and *Love Wins,* how the gospel is being modified – sometimes distorted out of all recognition – by some within the church under the pressures of contemporary society (and in particular the ideas in and around the agenda of political correctness). Yes, the church can change its style to adapt to the culture, but it is not to change the message. In these two books we have witnessed attempts to change things which should never be changed.

Secular grace?

In closing this chapter, let me just broaden things out a little to the influence of the wider culture on individual Christians. We are not talking here about books which attempt to change our doctrinal standards, but we are thinking about the way ordinary believers are swayed in their thinking by society at large, and in particular by the ubiquitous TV.

US TV shows are not among my personal favourites, but they are extremely popular. Certainly, series like *Scrubs* and *Glee* are *de rigueur* for most twenty- and thirty-somethings.

These shows regularly promote the friendly face of what we might call 'secular grace'. The ethos is very PC, very therapy culture. It is one in which everyone is accepted. That is absolutely right when it comes to such matters as race or disability or gender. But the agenda of these shows is more generally to do with morality. Especially it is to do with sexual morality. As we have now noted many times in this book, in today's secular society of tacit atheism, morals are relative, a matter of opinion. We are all aware of our own failures. So the mantra is, we do not judge anyone. We just accept – like grace.

Pushing the envelope

You find this secular grace, allied to political correctness, running through TV series like *Friends*, *Sex in the City*, *House* and all the way back to *M.A.S.H.* If you want to follow the trail on this, the book *Primetime Propaganda* by Ben Shapiro, subtitled 'How the Left took over your TV' would be a worthwhile read. Shapiro's thesis is that there is no organised conspiracy, but that creative people tend to be liberal in outlook and are drawn to work in a creative medium like TV. Being liberal and PC and seeing traditional morality and family life as restrictive to self-expression and therefore, in their terms, an 'evil' in society, they have tried to 'make a difference'. So they produce light entertainment which subtly questions and undermines the old standards. Audiences laugh along as their viewing pushes the envelope on moral issues.

The point we need to address is this. For many people, this secular grace is seen as more 'gracious' than God's grace. It not only accepts people as they are, it does not try to change them. This is viewed as true kindness. Within this liberal ethos, the gospel is made to look narrow and the church comparatively unloving. It is these kinds of pressures which *Love Wins* and *The Shack* were reacting to and have compromised with. This propaganda is a large influence today and closes many minds to the gospel. If they have not thought the issue through, it also makes many ordinary Christians feel awkward around their secular friends. But it is a lie.

The cost

Over the years, we have talked about this a number of times at home among the family. Here are some of the things which have emerged from our post-TV-watching conversations.

First, the makers of secular grace TV shows give the impression that morals are totally relative. But even they will draw the lines somewhere. Is paedophilia okay? Are terrorists to be accepted? How about consensual cannibalism? The answer would be 'no'. They do not believe that morals are actually relative. They have simply redrawn the line to suit themselves. They too are 'narrow' in their outlook. The impression that they are very 'all-accepting' while Christianity is not is untrue. They are very accepting of people like themselves, but when it comes to religious people, especially Christian people, they are not accepting at all. That is why you rarely find any Christian characters in these shows; or if you do, they are simply there to be caricatured and made fun of. Their claim to be more gracious than God is hypocrisy.

Second, those who push the envelope of moral issues rarely show the results of taking their advice. For example, the serious consequences of sexually transmitted diseases are not mentioned. The trauma and tears brought to children of marriages which break up through adultery are not part of the plot. The misery of women battling to make ends meet as single mothers and the statistics concerning the way children from broken homes are disadvantaged play no part in the script.

Third, the idea that secular grace is more loving than God's grace is a lie because secular grace costs nothing. It does not cost one leper to accept another leper. It would be hypocritical not to do so. It does not cost a sinner to receive other sinners. But God is not a sinner. He does not have to accept us. He is holy and has every right to reject us. But he does not. Instead, he paid for our sins in the person of Christ at the cross. And it cost Jesus everything. That is true grace.

Those who wish to change the gospel in order to satisfy the amoral outlook of contemporary society are missing the point. The immensity of God's holiness, through the cross of Christ, has become the measure of the enormous magnitude of his love.

What we need to be declaring to our lost world is summed up beautifully in Matthew Henry's memorable words: 'You have a holy God above you, a precious soul within you, and an awful eternity before you.' Therefore, we would add, you need a loving Saviour beside you.

Chapter 11
What happened to tolerance?

Four days after 9/11, arch-atheist Professor Richard Dawkins blamed the tragedy on what he called 'religion'.

Religion, he said, is 'a ready-made system of mind control which has been honed over the centuries' and 'teaches the dangerous nonsense that death is not the end'. It is ideally suited to brainwashing 'testosterone-sodden young men too unattractive to get a woman in this world ... desperate enough (referring to Islamic teaching about 'martyrdom') to go for seventy two private virgins in the next'. By holding out the promise of an afterlife, religion devalues this life and makes the world 'a very dangerous place'.

Since then, of course, Professor Dawkins has gone on to become a kind of 'evangelist for atheism', giving lectures attacking religion – and particularly Christianity – in many places. His book *The God Delusion* has become an international best-seller.

Soon after 9/11 and the initial attack on religion from Professor Dawkins, *The Guardian* newspaper columnist Polly Toynbee chimed in: 'The only good religion is a moribund religion: only when the faithful are weak are they tolerant and peaceful.' Similarly, Matthew Parris in the *Spectator* proposed that Christianity and Islam are both potentially violent because they both want to conquer the world and have a belief in an afterlife which puts the world to come before this one.

It is easy to understand such attacks on 'religion' following 9/11. People are rightly angered by what happened. They are, however, too politically correct, and anxious to avoid charges of 'Islamophobia'. So instead of laying the blame where it really belongs, they attack 'religion' generally, which is seen as more acceptable.

The New Testament specifically teaches that, though Christianity would love to 'conquer the world', we are specifically forbidden from using force of arms or threats to do so. Jesus said to Pilate, 'My kingdom is not of this world. If it were, my servants would fight...' (John 18:36). The Lord rebuked Peter for using a sword and said, 'Put your sword back in its place, for all who draw the sword will die by the sword' (Matt. 26:52). The apostle Paul often likens the Christian struggle to see the world saved to warfare, but he makes it very clear that this is merely a metaphor and that violence is to have no place in the Christian church. 'For though we live in the world, we do not wage war as the world does. The weapons we fight with are not the weapons of the world. On the contrary they have divine power to demolish strongholds. We demolish arguments and every pretension that sets itself up against the knowledge of God' (2 Cor. 10:3-5). The Christian warfare is through preaching, reasoning, love, prayer and care to win hearts and minds.

This is only too clear. Nevertheless, instead of the blame for suicide bombings, etc., being laid where it actually belongs – at the feet of radical Islam – somehow Christians have been brought into the picture, because (as a result of the pressures of political correctness) the problem is said to be 'religion' in general.

The myth of secular tolerance

Underlying the attacks on 'religion' by the prominent professors and newspaper columnists of the humanist-liberal establishment is what we might call 'the myth of secular tolerance'. This is that 'tolerance comes naturally to the secular person, whereas intolerance comes naturally to the religious believer'. It gives the impression that all religious believers are bigots and that secular people are somehow immune from the temptation to vilify or persecute people who do not see things their way and are different from them.

This idea is one which, as shall see, is built on very shaky foundations. Nevertheless, it is a kind of 'myth' which nourishes the current politically correct culture and has captured the mindset of the majority of people around us. What do Christians have to say in answer to this?

What is tolerance?

Before going any further, we need to be clear what we are talking about. What is tolerance? The most helpful definition is given by the philosopher Roger Scruton in his *Dictionary of Political Thought*. He defines tolerance as 'the policy of patient forbearance towards that which is not approved'. Tolerance is not the same as approval or indifference. The tolerant person exercises *restraint* towards something they actually dislike. A fuddy-duddy father may be said to tolerate his children's blaring rock music, for example, precisely because he dislikes it but refrains from banning it from the home. By contrast, intolerance involves the active attempt to suppress or silence whatever we disapprove of or do not agree with.

Of course, the means of suppression may vary. In Jerusalem, the Jews wanted the apostle Paul arrested and put to death, and plotted to kill him (Acts 23:12-13), whereas in Corinth they simply shouted him down (Acts 18:6) so that he had to leave the synagogue and rent a hall to teach in. It was different when Paul preached in Athens. Many of the philosophers simply laughed and sneered at him once he mentioned the resurrection, and did not give him a platform for his message again (Acts 17:32). So the way intolerance is expressed can go all the way from the use of state coercion and the death penalty, through to vitriol and character assassination, down to just being laughed at and given the cold shoulder. And in fact, if you think about the remarks from Richard Dawkins *et al* we quoted at the beginning of the chapter, the latter (vitriol, name-calling, stereotyping, etc.) is precisely what much of their polemics consists of.

The reality of secularism and political correctness

Secularism arose, in the eighteenth century, not firstly as a rejection of Christianity itself but as a rejection of the state church. The idea of a state church is something we do not find in the New Testament and is something that I (as a Baptist) have no wish to defend.

Interestingly, in his book *The Twilight of Atheism*, Alister McGrath brings a strong case that it is the countries which have had a state church (like the Church of England) where atheism is now most prevalent. It is as if people have reacted against feeling that Christianity is being forced upon them by the nation's constitution. Atheism is not first of all the inevitable result of the modern world and technological advance. The most advanced nation is the USA. But interestingly, it is still one of the most religious. That is because, McGrath argues, there has been a separation of church and state written into the laws of America since its inception. This has meant that religion is entirely voluntary (just as we find it in the New Testament). This has led, he argues, to it not suffering the same kind of decline that it has faced in other Western countries which have had state churches.

It was in response to what was seen as the oppression of state churches that secularism took off. People like Voltaire in France championed secularism against the oppressive control of the Catholic Church allied to the Royalty. (The state church in England also martyred many people under both Mary I and Elizabeth I.) These rationalists of the Enlightenment wanted toleration. They wanted to be able to think freely. Voltaire has a famous saying attributed to him about toleration: 'I disagree with what you say, but I will defend to the death your right to say it.' In many ways this is a positive legacy. Such thinking is necessary for a free society.

However, high ideals often give way to rougher tactics in the real world and such ideals were soon left behind.

- In France, soon after the Revolution of 1789 the secular revolutionaries launched the fiercely intolerant de-Christianization campaign during the 'Reign of Terror', with thousands of clergy and even nuns, as well as nobility, sent to the guillotine.
- The militant atheism of Karl Marx's followers was to

become the major source of the persecution of religious people (as well as many others) in the twentieth-century world. And of course, in Communist China that persecution by a secular/atheistic state still continues today.

The philosopher John Gray (himself a non-believer) has been honest enough to highlight the history of secular intolerance. 'The mass-murders of the twentieth century were not perpetrated by some latter day version of the Spanish Inquisition. They were done by atheist regimes in the service of Enlightenment ideas of progress. Stalin and Mao were not believers in original sin. Even Hitler, who despised Enlightenment values of equality and freedom, shared the Enlightenment faith that a new world could be created by human will. Each of these tyrants imagined that the human condition could be transformed through the use of science' (*New Statesman,* December 2002).

These plain facts of recent history flatly contradict the 'myth of secular tolerance' of Dawkins, Toynbee, Parris and others. Secular people can be just as intolerant as anyone else. People have 'utopian' ideas about how the world ought to be. They are so sure that they are right about this vision of 'the perfect state' that if some people have to be liquidated in order to achieve it, that does not matter. The end justifies the means. And secular people are just as vulnerable to this way of behaving as anyone else.

Political correctness

The rise of political correctness is actually an expression of secular intolerance. As we have seen, political correctness can be thought of as an outlook that classifies certain groups of people as victims in need of protection from criticism, so that no censure should be permitted against these groups, even if such criticism could be substantiated and argued reasonably.

The politically correct have decided that their support of those groups which they have identified as hard-done-by is so right that their ideas must be forced upon everyone else. I am not suggesting that PC will use the death penalty; but they are very much prepared to pass laws and bring in penalties to impose their will.

Already, with the passing of New Labour's Sexual Orientation Regulations, the freedom of religious believers to act according to their consciences has been over-ridden. It could well be that Christian teachers who refuse to teach that gay relationships are just as valid as heterosexual marriage will lose their jobs. Polly Toynbee has written that 'religion should be kept at home, in the private sphere'. The philosopher A. C. Grayling advocates the secularisation of society, which would mean 'that government funding for church schools and "faith-based" organisations…would cease, as would religious programming in public broadcasting'. Hence, Christians and others would become second-class citizens.

The reason secularism will always push in this direction is the exact reverse of the logic which Dawkins uses about the dangers of religion and belief in the afterlife. If you do not believe in an afterlife, then your perfect society has to be built in this world and there is no point waiting. The only time is now. So remove or side-line people who don't agree. 'You can't make an omelette without breaking a few eggs,' is the oft-quoted adage in such situations. Religious believers are the eggs. Hence the erosion of tolerance we are witnessing.

The Christian roots of toleration

What about the second component of the myth? This is the claim that intolerance is inbuilt and is inevitable in the religious believer. This is clearly the slur that is put around today.

It is an idea that is closely related to another myth. This is what we could call 'the myth of neutrality'. The idea is that somehow the secular person is not previously committed to any set of assumptions and is therefore able to weigh up a proposition in a fairer way than the person who is already committed religiously. But, of course, there is a fallacy here. The secular person is already committed to the idea that God either does not exist or is irrelevant to daily life. That is what makes him or her secular. Thus there is no way that they are neutral, especially when it comes to examining matters which might relate to spiritual things or evidence concerning God.

As we have already seen, we must not confuse tolerance of something with agreeing with it. Tolerance is precisely about living with something with which you do not agree. Historically we find, actually, that it was not first of all secular rationalists of the eighteenth century but Christian believers of the seventeenth century who forged the path of toleration. It was Christian people – in particular nonconformist Christians – who were the first advocates of a 'live and let live' attitude towards those of differing religious points of view. Back in the sixteenth century, both Edward VI (in 1549) and Elizabeth I (1559) brought forward laws which proposed that only worship according to the Church of England's *Book of Common Prayer* would be legal. Many Christians felt that this was too restrictive. The Puritan movement arose against this background. The Pilgrim Fathers left Britain for the New World over this matter of freedom of religious expression, and many of the troubles between the King and Parliament which sadly led to the English Civil War were centred around the same issue. When Oliver Cromwell became the Protector of England, after Parliament won the Civil War, he brought a degree of toleration. Nonconformist Christian worship was allowed. The Jews had been expelled from England in 1290 in the reign of King Edward I. In 1656, under the Cromwellian Protectorate, they were readmitted. But when the Protectorate failed with the death of Cromwell, things changed back. The Act of Uniformity (1662) was an Act of the Parliament of England under Charles II, which required the use of all the rites and ceremonies in the Book of Common Prayer in Church of England services. It also required ordination by a Church of England bishop for all ministers. As a result, nearly 2,000 clergymen left the established church in what became known as the Great Ejection. The Test and Corporation Acts, which lasted until 1828, excluded all nonconformists from holding civil or military office. Nonconformists were also prevented from being awarded degrees by the universities of Cambridge and Oxford. So it is clear that the struggle for tolerance was going on long before secularism really appeared on the scene. This ought to be enough in itself to scotch the idea that religious people are naturally intolerant. It was initially religious people who fought for toleration.

But further, their case against intolerance and persecution was fundamentally Biblical and theological. They became convinced that coercion in religion was a betrayal of the gospel. Here are four strands of their thinking.

1) The mercy of God

The good news of Jesus reveals that we are all the objects of divine tolerance, of God's mercies. Why is the world not destroyed? Despite our sin and rebellion against him, God the Father displays an almost incredible longsuffering towards us. 'Because of the LORD's great love we are not consumed, for his compassions never fail. They are new every morning; great is your faithfulness' (Lam. 3:22-23). He postpones the day of judgement, endures our hostility and offers us forgiveness (2 Peter 3:9). Like the father of the prodigal son, he longs for our return to his embrace. Those arguing for toleration said that Christians, who are so indebted to God for his tolerance towards them all the years they resisted Christ, ought to display mercy and patience towards others. How great is God's forbearance! 'God demonstrates his own love for us in this: While we were still sinners [in rebellion against God], Christ died for us' (Rom. 5:8; brackets mine).

2) The teaching of Christ

Secondly, it was pointed out that the tolerance of the Father is reflected in the teaching and life of Jesus. He is meek and lowly, riding into Jerusalem on a donkey, not a warhorse; persecuted, but never persecuting. His Sermon on the Mount enjoins Christians to love their enemies. Luke 9:51-56 tells us that when his disciples wanted to call down fire from heaven on a Samaritan village which had refused to give him hospitality, he rebuked them.

3) The Nature of Evangelism

It is true that we want to conquer the world for Christ – but not by coercion or persecution like other religions. As we have already noted in this chapter, our warfare is spiritual (2 Cor. 10:3-5). The kingdom grows through prayer and preaching and persuasion, not by violence. It is about winning hearts, not winning gun battles and shoot-outs.

4) The Certainty of Heaven

At his trial, Jesus confessed to Pilate that he was a king (John 18:35-37). But his kingdom is not of this world, it is of the world to come. And it comes to him 'from another place' (that is, from God), and therefore it is certain. Therefore, he and his followers do not have wage war in this world. Our weapon is simply truth.

The determination to break with the idea of the state church and return to New Testament principles brought remarkable results, which by 1700 led to the break-down of the enforcement of many religious laws in this country and later led to freedom of religion and tolerance in the New World of the United States. The idea that Christians are naturally intolerant is downright wrong. Paradoxically, the modern commitment to tolerance arose from the attempts by Christian religious dissenters and others to enact New Testament principles. The myth of secular tolerance is a propaganda weapon against Christianity; but it is not true.

Recommended reading:

D. A. Carson, *The Intolerance of Tolerance* (Leicester: IVP, 2012)

Postscript

This book has tried to show how the tacit atheism of our present time is leading society astray and tying us into knots through our own foolishness. Perhaps the following poem, relating imagined events at Speakers' Corner in London, sums up how atheism will always rebound on its perpetrators.

'There is no God,' the speaker cries
'Don't let your thoughts be chained;
This universe evolved itself,
This world is self-contained.'

Just then, an urchin in the crowd
A skilful pebble throws,
Which accurately lands upon,
His atheistic nose.

'Who threw that stone?' the speaker roars;
At which, a cockney elf,
Intuitively keen, retorts,
'No one! It frew itself.'

So a pathetic casualty,
Discomfited, and worse,
Goes home to meditate upon
This causeless Universe!
> S. J. Forrest, *Time for a Rhyme*

Meditating on the opening lines of *The Shorter Catechism*, which tells us that 'Man's chief end is to glorify God, and to enjoy him forever,' the great Puritan Thomas Watson comments concerning atheism that a man 'had better lose his life than the end of his living' (*A Body of Divinity*).